REFLECTIONS *of an* ISLAND GIRL

I hope the love of the Lake & her islands grow + grow inside of you!

6.30.25

-Ch

Design and production:
Foster Design Collaborative

Cover illustration:
Peggy Tuttle

Manufactured in the United States of America
First Edition
10 9 8 7 6 5 4 3 2 1

ISBN 978-1-63752-241-7

Christine L. Ontko
PO Box 507
Put-in-Bay OH 43456

Freshwater Retreat
⊕ freshwaterretreat.com
✉ freshwatersensations@yahoo.com

REFLECTIONS *of an* ISLAND GIRL

CHRISTINE L.ONTKO

Dedicated to my daughters, Anna and Meredith,
sixth generation Island Girls. I love you both
to the moon, the stars, the galaxies, and back.

Home is the nicest word there is.
Laura Ingalls Wilder

CONTENTS

CONTENTS (cont.)

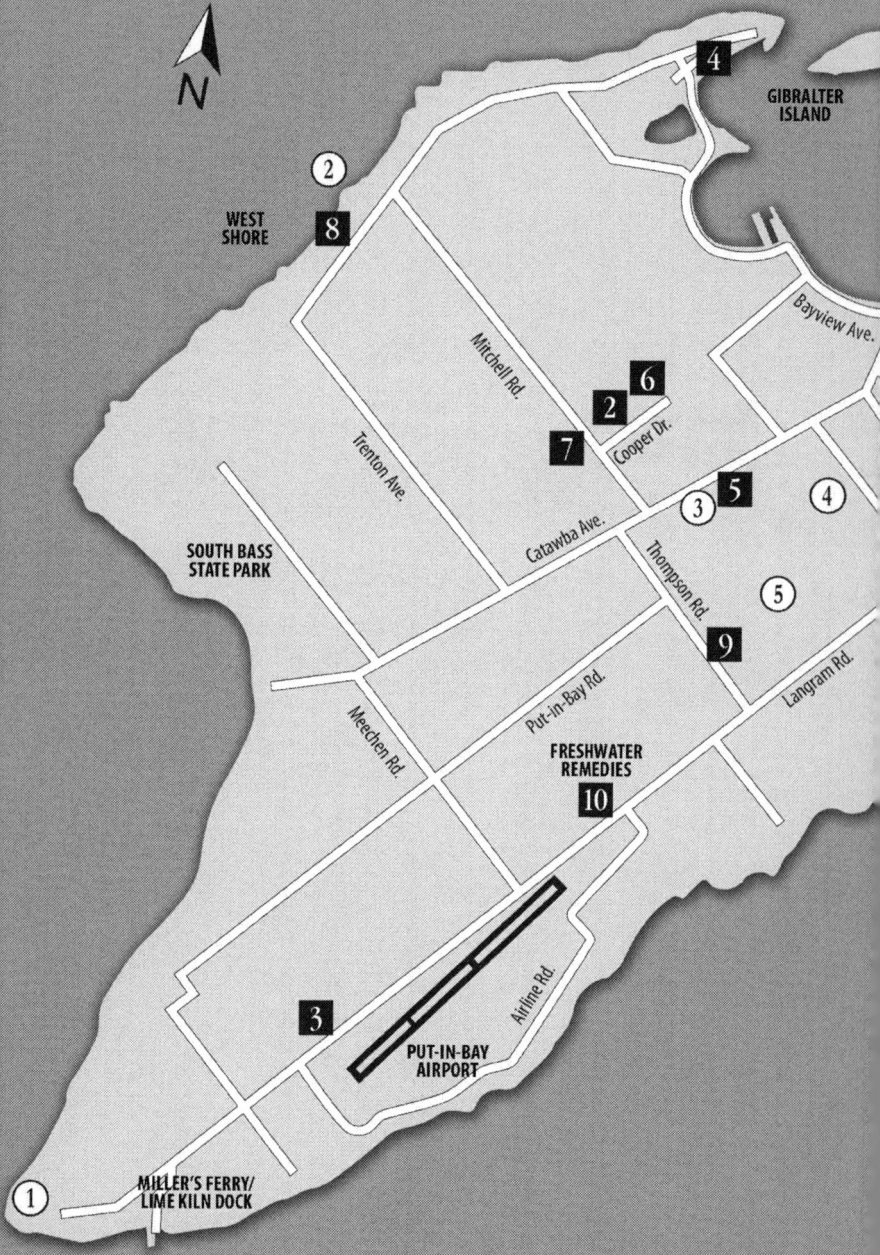

N

GIBRALTER
ISLAND

④

WEST
SHORE

②

⑧

Bayview Ave.

Mitchell Rd.

② ⑥

Trenton Ave.

⑦ Cooper Dr.

③ ⑤ ④

SOUTH BASS
STATE PARK

Catawba Ave.

Thompson Rd.

⑤

⑨

Put-in-Bay Rd.

Meechen Rd.

Langram Rd.

FRESHWATER
REMEDIES

⑩

③

Airline Rd.

PUT-IN-BAY
AIRPORT

①

MILLER'S FERRY/
LIME KILN DOCK

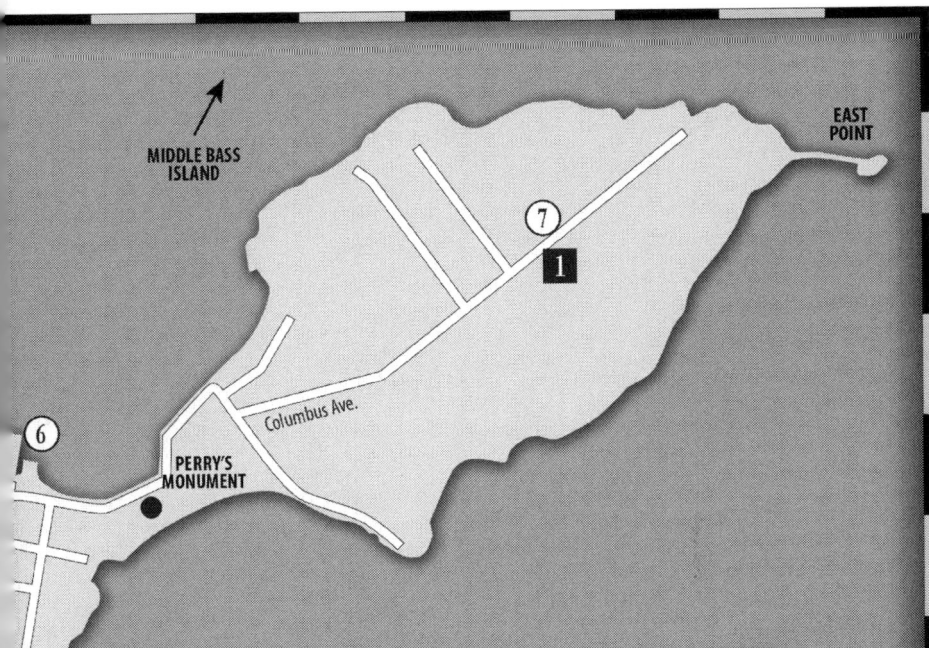

MIDDLE BASS
ISLAND

EAST
POINT

Columbus Ave.

PERRY'S
MONUMENT

SOUTH BASS ISLAND

(a.k.a. Put-in-Bay)

1. Lighthouse Point (f.k.a. Parker's Point)
2. Sunset Ramp
3. The Goat
4. Cooper's Hill
5. Shady Path
6. Jet Express (f.k.a. Parker Boat Line)
7. Cummings House

1 – 10

Christie's 10 different homes on the
island (in chronological order)

FOREWORD

I WAS THRILLED WHEN CHRISTIE Ontko asked me to write the foreword to her book. I love anything written about the Lake Erie Islands.

Like a puff of wind filling the spinnaker of a sailboat, Christie takes you into the world of a fifth-generation "Islander." It is a journey that one relishes because the root of great writing comes from the heart. Christie has a big heart and her writing carries the authority and experience of a unique place, Put-in-Bay.

Her perspective, based on over four decades of "Island Living" and a family arsenal of stories that goes back to the 1860's, gives the reader a glimpse of the evolution of the Lake Erie Islands.

Christie is a graduate of Put-in-Bay High School (1991) and, armed with a teaching degree from Bowling Green State University (1995), she taught elementary school for the Put-in-Bay school district. Her students came from South Bass, Middle Bass, and North Bass but her fame has stretched beyond her home island because of her writing.

Frequent guests to her writing include her daughters, Anna and Meredith. They are sixth-generation Islanders and enjoyed many of the rights of passage that Christie did. Ice Cake Jumping (Darwinian in nature), bonfires blazing incongruously on the ice in the middle of Put-in-Bay harbor, and the graffiti signing of the rear walls of the townhall theatre after the last performance of that year's show.

Other subjects include her mother Linda's magic pantry which, even in the depths of winter, contained arcane and unusual ingredients for even the most obscure baking need. Captain Alf "The Old Man" Parker, Charlie Tuna, Parker Point, Cliff "Ice Man" Fulton, Annie Parker, Christie's laying hens, the *Yankee Clipper*, and the Erie Isles ferries also make appearances.

Christie and I were fortunate to write for Jeff Koehler, editor of the Put-in-Bay *Gazette*. In 2013 we did a roast of Jeff and his 33 years at the helm of the *Gazette* (the rumors of cannibalism were not true). Here is Christie's toast:

> It is just amazing to write for Jeff and the *Gazette*! He is just that cool. He lets me use the word "that" too often, as well as write in a style that's not always grammatically correct. I love that about that guy! I love that he allows me to be published. I love that I can fulfill a childhood dream of being a writer just like Laura Engalls Wilder from the *Little House on the Prairie* books!

I once joked to Christie that Jeff was paying me $1,000 per article. Not to be outdone, she responded without hesitation that she was being paid $1,200 per article and enjoyed the use of a Mercedes-Benz Smart car on the *Gazette* tab…. The irony is that *Gazette* writers are unpaid.

I grew up on Middle Bass Island during the summers, and one of my favorite residents was Anna Kuemmel (Christie's great-grandmother). I owe my lifelong obsession with boats to her. She lent me the pram that her children had used while growing up. At the age of four, I was knocking about "Gramma K's" marina with strict instructions not to go outside the marina's boundaries or I would be taken by a Kraken. Germans can be so dramatic about their sea monsters. It was Gramma Kuemmel's Middle Bass diaries that inspired Christie to be a writer.

I always looked forward to the first of the month when the Put-in-Bay *Gazette* would arrive. However, I noticed that the crisp folds of the paper were frequently smudged and the pages curled. Investigation revealed that my office manager, Annette Kinder, was intercepting the paper to read Christie's column. "I love her stories! Her columns are like *Little House on the Prairie*, but better!" Mission accomplished, Christie!

I bought Annette her own subscription to the *Gazette* so my copy would remain unmolested—a quirk of my character.

Here is your fresh copy of Christie's stories. Like rich chocolates, each chapter is a sweet literary treat full of surprises.

Gordy Barr
January 21, 2021

Gordon Barr is a columnist for the Put-in-Bay *Gazette* and the author of two books: *Middle Bass & Other Lake Erie Islands* and *Wine Bass Island Stories*. He is currently working on his third, but certainly not his last.

ACKNOWLEDGMENTS

WHERE WOULD I BE without the love of my parents? Special thanks go out to my mom who has books upon books of our family history in photos, neatly organized in albums. She has always put up with my creative ideas and endless questions about our family. Mom, thanks for being patient with me and allowing me to be myself. Dad, thank you for being the biggest cheerleader any daughter could ask for. Even when life has gotten me down, you've always been there to tell me it'll be okay.

Many thanks go to my partner, Cliff Fulton, for encouraging my writing and always giving me something to write about. Gordon Barr, island friend, thanks for your persistence in getting me to publish these stories! Without your extra gentle nudges, I may not have done so. You also introduced me to Peggy Tuttle, the editor of all these li'l stories, a kind woman who helped guide me throughout this process.

My deepest gratitude goes out to Mainland Jen and my many island friends, for without all of you to share life experiences, I wouldn't have these stories! Thank you all so much.

Christie Ontko
March 4, 2021

The following stories were written
over a period of nearly ten years,
while writing my column,
"Island Girl"
for the Put-in-Bay *Gazette*.

1

THE HORRIBLE ISLANDER

I AM A HORRIBLE ISLANDER. I never remember the boat schedule, and don't even ask me if they're running today or not because I won't know the answer. Even though my father and grandfather were both ferry boat captains, I simply do not know this information. Grandpa Alfred Parker would "turn over in his grave" (a term my mother often uses) if he knew that his granddaughter didn't know what it meant when we get a Nor'easter. I hear this term from time to time, but I really don't know if that means the water level goes down, or up, or if the boats will run, or *what*! I just know it's bad when we get a Nor'easter. I also know that when this happened when I was young, my sister Natalie, brother Davey, Mom and Dad, and I would all pile in my mom's '53 Chevy and go for a ride to see the storm.

Another example is that my attitude is so crummy when I want to get off the island and can't. Maybe it's the wind, or fog, or whatever—but when I can't get *outta here* when I want to, I'm not a nice person to be around. Oh, many of you know me as "ye old nice-and-kind school teacher, Miss Christie," but many of you haven't seen me when I am ready to shop at T.J. Maxx, and I can't because there are no boats, or planes, or a bridge. Not a pretty sight. Just ask my husband, Cliff—he has seen this side of me. Or you could ask my best friend, "Mainland Jen," who is waiting for me on the other side with money in her purse and ready to shop, right along with me.

When guests arrive at my home on Thompson Rd., questions always follow. I can handle a question like "How many students are in the school?" But anything more than that, and I feel like a loser on *Jeopardy!* I remember the first summer when Cliff's dad, Roger, came for a visit. When he arrived, he began asking me questions about my family's history. All I knew was that my grandpa operated a ferry boat line, and along with my grandma, Elizabeth, they worked hard each day to make the business a success. I knew that my Uncle Joe Parker was one of the kindest men Put-in-Bay has ever known. Well, Roger is a computer whiz, and he had done his research, so he began telling me about how the Parkers owned the property where the lighthouse stands today and that it was called "Parker's Point." He was shocked to see my surprise when I heard this information. He has since filled me in on lots of island lore, and I'm continuing to learn about Put-in-Bay history every time he visits.

Another thing I do not know is how to clean fish—I only know that you have to cut the heads off first. The whole scene just horrifies me. When I was young, I made a habit of letting those adorable silver minnows (which were meant for bait) swim free when I went ice-fishing with my dad, Charlie Tuna. What I *do* know about fish is that no one can top the taste of my late Aunt Christine's fried perch. Salted, of course!

I never stock up on enough food. In the fall, I spend at least two teachers' salaries on supplies but come January, I simply have nothing left in my pantry. How does my mom do it so well? Her cupboards are like Mary Poppins' magic bag. Amazing things can be found in Mary's bag, and it's just like that in Mom's numerous cupboards. If I need to bake gingerbread cookies and I need molasses, well then, I just get in the car and drive the half-mile to my mom's house to find it. Mom's got it all. Maybe that's why I never learned.

Why do I write this silly nonsense? Because sometimes it makes me realize that maybe I'm not so horrible at being an Islander after all. When I got home from school today, a fresh snow had fallen. I didn't have anywhere to be except here. I wasn't upset about a plane possibly not flying, or a boat not running, or my imaginary bridge not being built. But instead, I used the beautiful winter day to take my dog, Fair, for a walk. I walked down the street, never worrying about my safety or getting salt on my new leather boots. I knew every person in each car that passed me. I left the back door unlocked when I left home, and the car sat in my driveway with the keys in the ignition. I realized that even though I don't know the boat schedule, how to clean fish, or stock my cupboards sufficiently, I do know all about the beauty of Put-in-Bay and all who choose to call it home. Just when I think I should have my Islander card revoked, I realize that I am allowed to hold it tight. That is, until I want to shop at T.J. Maxx and can't get there.

Gramma K. cleaning fish, Middle Bass

2

THE ICE WALKER

WHEN CLIFF AND I first began our courtship, he was living and working in Columbus, and I was living on Put-in-Bay. We didn't think much about transportation issues in our relationship because it was mid-summer, and the boats always ran on time. Sometimes we were lucky, and there was another one thrown in, and he would arrive ten minutes sooner than expected.

With the wind in his face and his tie blowing ever so romantically over his shoulder, Cliff cherished the serene 18-minute boat ride over to the quiet island. So did all the young girls heading over to celebrate their upcoming weddings, dressed in bachelorette attire. One young soon-to-be-bride batted her false eyelashes at him and commented, "You're awfully dressed up for Put-in-Bay." He didn't even look at her [yeah right] but simply nodded and responded, "I'm going to see my girlfriend."

Trudging up the long hill in 90-degree heat, he would arrive with roses in one hand and a loaf of really good bread in the other. I'm not talking about just any bread, but the whole grain kind that you can only buy at IGA. No offense to Greg Hughes, owner of the Island General Store. His bread is great, but Catawba IGA's organic bread is my favorite. There would be my man, in full suit and tie, courting me with roses and organic wheat bread. Now, does it get any better than that?

Summer quickly became fall, and the weather grew colder. Cliff had seen that I had a fireplace, but no firewood, so he thought he would be a gentleman and chop some. Since single girls don't normally have axes with which to cut firewood, he bought one on the mainland. Well, one fall evening, Cliff arrived via the *Jet Xpress* ferry late on a Friday night, riding with various late-night visitors. With an axe slung over his shoulder and wearing his black suit with a red satin tie, a tourist asked him, "I hope you're not going to the island to kill someone?"

"No," Cliff responded, "I'm going to see my girlfriend."

We never considered the upcoming winter and possible frustrations with travel. The thought had actually occurred to me, but as quickly as it did, I ushered it out of my mind. I didn't want to think of anything ruining the wonderful relationship we were building. And, on top of all of that, he was now bringing me fresh produce and other goodies! I knew all too well what could happen in the winter months. Wind, snow, fog, and other uncontrollable forces can prevent transportation to and from the island, wreaking havoc with relationships and weekend plans.

Sadly, the boats did stop running that fall, as they always do. Couldn't just *one* year the darn things run all year long? Where was my bridge? Because now was a really good time to have one! I mean, what was I going to eat with my eggs in the morning—*normal* bread? Where was I going to get my supply of fresh berries and Greek yogurt? I had gotten so spoiled by all the mainland stuff that Cliff would bring me, and I was beginning to wonder, "Am I dating him for the groceries?"

After Cliff had flown with Dairy Air Bob for the first time, I found out that people on the island thought someone had died. Was it the suit and tie he wore? Did he look like he was in mourning when he came to visit me? Another time they thought that he was my attorney. But fortunately, no one had died, and I had no need for an attorney…at that time.

The winter weather got so bitter cold that year that the ice had formed solidly across the lake. It was so good, in fact, that ice fishermen were lined up all along Catawba Point, clear across the channel to Put-in-Bay. One very cold winter, my family had traveled by ice across the channel in my mom's '53 Chevy to visit my Grandma Ontko in Marblehead. That's the only time in all my life I have traveled via the channel on the lake to the mainland. In fact, I was always taught that you should never trust the ice on the channel because the current could eat away at the bottom layer, and you could never be sure how thick it really was.

Cliff was to arrive that weekend. It was Thursday evening when I got the usual call from him telling me what time to expect him the following day.

He said to me, "I think I'm going to walk over. From dock to dock."

"On the ice?" I asked in disbelief. "You can't walk across the ice! It's the channel." I knew the ice could be a place of fun and fishing, but sadly, I have also seen the perils the frozen lake has brought to our small island communities.

"Well, when I flew in last week, I saw tons of shanties all the way over. It looked like there were even tracks from Lime Kiln Dock to Catawba." Cliff responded.

I was so proud of him; he was even using the correct terms like "Lime Kiln Dock."

"Plus," he continued, "the weather is supposed to be calm tomorrow—no snow or wind. But cold. Good for the ice."

"Let me call John Dodge and my mom," I said. [I always call

my mom and my neighbor for advice on such island things.]
"I'll call you back in ten minutes."

Even though Cliff had never walked on frozen Lake Erie
because he was a mainlander, I also knew him well enough
to know that once he sets his mind to something, there is no
changing it. He was an adventurer who had traversed the des-
erts of Saudi Arabia and the jungles of Panama. It was as if I
were Millie—famously, Put-in-Bay's only deer—and he was a
mainland buck. Nothing was going to stop him.

I called him back exactly ten minutes later, telling him I
had heard that many others were traveling via the channel, but
I had some simple rules for him:

#1. He must wear creepers.

#2. He must call me before leaving and, lastly...

#3 Text me every ten minutes of his journey.

The next day was Friday, and he planned his trip during
my lunch hour from school so that I could pick him up and
be in constant communication with him. At about 12:45, I sat
in my Chevy Cavalier at the end of Miller's Lime Kiln Dock,
awaiting my love.

Cliff had journeyed the miles across the frozen lake, and
upon meeting his last ice fisherman, the question was asked of
him, "What are you doing walking out here? Lost something?"

With metal creepers attached to his boots and phone in
hand, he simply responded, "I'm going to see my girlfriend."

DISCLAIMER:

Do not attempt to walk across the lake—unless, of course, you
are a mainlander in love...or a deer.

3

THE OLD MAN

PEOPLE REFERRED TO MY grandfather, Alfred Parker, as "The Old Man," which is Naval slang for the captain of a ship. Even my parents called him that, which always shocked me. At a young age, we accompanied my mom to our family business, Parker Boat Line...*a lot*! We even took naps there on the twin beds back in the office. I have recently found out those beds were put there so Grandpa Alfred and his wife, Grandma Elizabeth, could sleep there and not have to go home at night.

Parker Boat Line was a ferryboat service that ran from downtown Put-in-Bay to the harbor in Port Clinton, hauling passengers, cars, and the island freight. As a young child, we often traveled the hour-and-a-half boat ride (for free, of course!) to the mainland for doctors' appointments, groceries, or banking. I remember one such ride that wasn't so wonderful.

"Get in the car! I told The Old Man we'd be there in ten minutes, and we're already late!" Linda yelled as her three children climbed into the midnight black '53 Chevy. The engine turned over smoothly in the old car, and they were on their way to the boat dock. They only lived about a mile away but sometimes living close by on an island wasn't a good thing. Could it be that some islanders can't tell time (some refer to this as "island time")? Or is it just that living on an island makes one think they've always got an extra five minutes?

As they pulled in, Alfred was already on the boat waiting for them. "Hurry up, damn it! I gotta go—the weather's changin' fast!" he hollered through the terrible spring winds.

They all walked the gangplank to the boat and knew right where to go. Linda took her usual seat in the captain's cabin, setting her heavy purse down and heaving a sigh of relief. The boat was rocking and rolling even in the dock, so she knew this would be a rough trip.

The three kids ran below to the engine room of the ferry and grabbed a soda pop. Christie picked a Red Pop, Davey an orange Fanta, and Natalie, who was still pretty young, copied her sister. The sodas fizzed open, and they had to quickly slurp some down so they wouldn't spill with the rolling of the ferry.

Next, they hit the candy bars. A Reese's peanut butter cup for Christie, a Hershey's plain chocolate bar for Davey, and for young Natalie, M&Ms. Sneaking their bites, they hurried up the steps to the pilothouse to join their mom and Grandpa.

Grandpa Parker always let them pick out a candy bar and pop when they boarded the *Erie Isle* ferry. It made the long hour-and-a-half trip more bearable. They didn't get sweets at home much, so going for a boat ride was exciting and a yummy treat for all three of them. Plus, Alfred made a bit of money from selling the concessions to tourists, so he could afford to give away some free ones to his grandkids.

As the engines roared and the boat backed out of the dock, everyone on board noticed the force of the winds on the ferry that day. Normally, tourists were on deck to watch the seagulls flying or the waves rush against the bow; however, today was not one of those days. Loudly and fiercely, the waves banged against the boat. The lake would carry the boat low, and then with a giant rolling motion, force the heavy ferry up high again on top of the waves.

Alfred was always dressed in a white shirt, dark pants, and tie—no matter what the conditions. Whether it was 32 degrees and there was ice in the bay, or if it was 95 degrees with high humidity, he dressed the part of a professional captain in charge of his ferryboats. Today was no different. As he held tight to the round wooden helm, the waves banged up hard against the bow of the boat. In and out, he tacked among the waves in an attempt to ease the gentle beast of a boat through the rough seas. Easing her into the high waves was what he had been taught. He wouldn't allow the lake to win this battle. He always won.

Linda didn't particularly enjoy the rough ride, but she was strong like her father and held her three kids close as they swayed with each roll. About halfway through the ride, Christie announced, "Mom, I think I'm gonna be sick."

"Get to the deck!" She said as gently as possible, grabbing her child by the hand.

"Mom, the boat's so rough!"

"Keep your eyes on the horizon." She walked her middle child to the back deck of the giant boat, the location where it was the most calm. Linda grabbed the five-gallon bucket the deckhands used for washing and turned it over for a make-shift seat. "Now, sit. And keep your eyes on the horizon. Don't watch the waves."

"But I can't see the horizon..." Christie had barely spat out those words when she felt that awfully familiar feeling in her stomach. Up came the Red Pop and the Reese's peanut butter cups. Thank God for the waves, as they were able to wash away the mess on the deck.

This is just one of many rough boat rides I recall as a child. I still get seasick to this day. You'd think that by now I'd have some kind of natural immunity to it: my grandpa, my father, and now my husband—all boat captains. However, I'm not so fortunate. Today, when on a rough boat ride, I have to sit in a certain part of the boat, put my head down, and breathe in fresh air to avoid puking all over the place.

Growing up on an island in Lake Erie has had its share of excitement. I never knew just how fascinating the life I've led was until now. I did know I was a bit different—not too many people can say they've lived on an island their whole life—but I can. Growing up on Put-in-Bay has been a unique experience. I began my first summer job as a tour guide at Perry's Cave. I was ten at the time and had to break away from being the shy little girl I was in order to parade 25 adults on a cave tour, all while remembering the 15-minute speech. During those tours, I'd get the regular tourist questions asked of me, such as "What's it like in the winter here?" "How many are in your school?" "What do your parents do for a living?"

The island's claim to fame is that the Battle of Lake Erie, won by Commodore Oliver Hazard Perry during the War of 1812, was fought just off our shores. My island ancestors have "quite a reputation," so I hear. My great-great-grandpa first arrived via Quebec, Canada. Gambling debts, along with the fact that his wife was from a well-to-do royalty-like family who disapproved of the marriage, inspired the Parker family to move from London, England to the New World. My great-great-grandpa was a fur trader in Canada and the United States. He had a few run-ins with the law and, for about a year, he was put into a Canadian prison while all the time his family thought he was dead! He returned home to the relief of his wife and then made an honest living working in the vineyards. He eventually ended up owning about half of Put-in-Bay. The area in which the lighthouse is located is still called Parker's Point.

During prohibition, one of my great uncles was involved in smuggling moonshine from the Canadian islands near Put-in-Bay. Yes, my family has had a crazy history!

With these roots on this island, there has to be a family business involved. For my family, it was a ferry company and a cave. Yes, a cave. Becoming a tour guide at the cave was the first job we grandchildren were allowed to work. We could also help down at the ferry dock. If you were a boy, you could work as a deckhand on the boats. As a female, I could sit in the office and help tabulate the figures and count the money. But not wanting to sit in the office all day, I chose the cave.

When I turned ten, in the early 80's I couldn't wait to start my first summer job! I begged my parents to let me, and reluctantly they did. Having followed my older brother down the steep concrete steps of the cave every day in the summers before, I already knew the speech just by listening. That tenth summer of my life was very memorable. Each day I packed a small lunch and bought a candy bar at the ticket counter with my extra tip money. I made $1.25 an hour and dreamed of all the things I could buy with a week's wages.

Now, our family businesses have all been sold, and I'm currently a teacher on the island as well as an entrepreneur myself. With the help of family and lots of faith, Freshwater Sensations, LLC opened in 2012 and is thriving. I can't believe I'm still here. I always said I'd move off after graduating from high school and teach in a warm, sunny place. But, as the famous saying goes, "There's no place like home."

4

THE WALKMAN

O N OUR LITTLE ISLAND, we are all beginning another year, and I cringe when I hear someone speak the date, "Twenty twelve." Let's just say "Two thousand twelve," it just sounds better and much less threatening. So many changes have happened here in recent years. Bars filled with water and sand (swim-up bars and ones with sand floors) have both been built. Tony's is now Tony's Garage, and Harbor Village is Harbor Square again. However, much seems to remain the same. Aren't we supposed to be having all our food materialize before our eyes by now, like in *Star Trek*? And just like that old cartoon, *The Jetsons*, shouldn't our form of transportation be a little floating car that can take us to the mainland whenever we wish, regardless of the weather conditions? Is life just flying by with changes everywhere, or is life remaining the same?

I know I'm not old enough to be saying this, but I will anyway. Back in my day, the island was so different. I remember when we called that giant hill "Cooper's Hill" because The Goat restaurant wasn't there yet, but instead, there was a place called Cooper's—that wonderful restaurant owned and operated by the Urge family, where they made the most delectable fried mushrooms ever! The cliffs along the West Shore were available to all of us to swim and jump off of during the summer, without having to walk around a "Private—No Swimming" sign. Lastly, I could mail a letter to a person on the island as "Local" without the silliness of a P.O. Box…and it would actually get to that person! What happened to the good ol' days?

Changes do and must occur. Lately, I've been noticing changes in my daughters, especially my youngest daughter, Meredith. She is thirteen now and growing what seems to be an inch every day, with the proof being in those large feet of hers. She has been borrowing my shoes (a size 9.5) since last spring. She has the Parker feet, poor kid. What's going on here? How is it that my youngest child is thirteen years old? It seems as if just yesterday I was graduating from college while my oldest daughter, Anna, was learning how to throw her first temper tantrum. Now, Anna is deciding her own path by picking out a college that suits her. How is it that my oldest child is graduating high school this year?

Anyway, back to Meredith. She recently just purchased an iPod. Saving the money she so dutifully earned this past summer, she acquired this little piece of musical technology. As we were driving to the Apple Store all the way over on the mainland in Westlake, I began telling my youngest about life: "Back in my day…."

I said with excitement, "I remember vividly saving up my babysitting money and really wanting the latest contraption—a Walkman!"

"A walk *what*?" Meredith asked.

"A Walkman," I simply said, as if she would know of such things. But what was I thinking? She probably didn't even know what a cassette tape was, let alone a device that could play only about ten songs, compared to the thousands her new iPod can hold. Also, my gadget couldn't even play all ten songs without the tape coming to an end and having to be manually flipped over. I didn't even dare bring up the archaic "record player." I continued, "Honey, a Walkman is just an older version of your iPod—that thing you are buying today to listen to music on."

A $250.00 iPod I did not have—instead, a much less expensive Sony Walkman. It arrived via Parker Boat Line (as did all our deliveries) after what seemed like a year of much anticipation. That day, I put my hair in pigtails as I rode my blue three-speed bike to the dock to pick it up. I can remember this day so vividly, partially because my Aunt Jeanette Luecke commented on my crooked pigtails, but more importantly because of my excitement about receiving my new Walkman!

That day on the way to the Apple Store with Meredith, I realized that maybe things really haven't changed that much in the past 25 years. It's just the *way* that life goes on that has changed so much. My social networking site wasn't called Facebook, but instead, it was called Tony's, our local hangout. We would all gather at Tony's and plan our next party. Merce Traverso was at the counter serving us pop and candy bars while we waited for our next turn at the pool table. I remember the song *Jack and Dianne* playing on the jukebox, along with the sounds of the bowling balls striking against the pins in the small bowling alley machine. All could be heard echoing loudly over the wooden floor of Tony's.

Today, when things seem to be so different, think about them from another viewpoint. The basic things in life truly remain the same. Like so many generations of Island Girls, Meredith is still enjoying the good life of Put-in-Bay, saving her money and spending a little. She eagerly anticipates the latest gadget to go on the market, and she spends her time socializing with friends. Not much different from my young life on the island.

During those teenage nights at Tony's, all I could think of was where I would go after high school graduation. I didn't realize that time would fly by so quickly. It is my New Year's wish that my children can live for the present and be truly grateful for all they have this very moment. I try to explain to my daughters that the good ol' days are *right now*! I hope they get it before I did. It took me years of constantly wishing for tomorrow to finally understand.

5

ICE CAKES

WHEN I LIVED ON that place we Islanders call the "mainland," I won't lie to you—things were very much more convenient. I know those mainlanders are trying to keep it a secret, but do you know that the UPS man delivers boxes right to your front door? Do you know that you can order a pizza in the winter? And it, like the UPS package, comes right to your house? I'm not kidding. These things happen. Like magic. Just as the mainlanders may take these things for granted, I sometimes take things for granted living here. I always have to be reminded of how unique and special my island life is, because I sometimes forget.

Our friend, Robert, visited us this winter from upstate New York, and he learned many new things about Put-in-Bay. Sure, he's visited during the summer months when the normal visitors arrive via ferry each half-hour, but coming in the wintertime was a first for him.

Robert was enthralled with all of our Island winter experiences. Such as the oxymoron of having a fire on the ice during our annual ice party at the end of January. When he saw this in person, he was dumbfounded. I thought nothing of this. All I was concerned about was keeping my fingertips warm by the fire on top of the frozen bay. I have grown up with ice parties, just as mainland children grow up with neighborhood block parties.

This winter has been a true Island winter, like the ones I remember as a child. My memory tells me that we had snow each year, plenty of ice fishing, and the blizzard of '78 seemed to last a month. I have memories of ice parties, just as we have all experienced this winter. The only thing that has changed is that Facebook now spreads the word about the ice parties, whereas, in 1983, word of mouth had to do. At those ice parties in the 1980's, I can recall the adults standing around socializing and sipping their libations while I ran around with my young friends in my moon boots, begging an adult to pull us on our sleds behind their snowmobiles.

Just as today, when I was a child, the public docks would fill with boats and partiers all summer long, but in the winter, they would often turn into an area of ice skating and ice cake jumping [or are they saying ice "keg" jumping?]. Many main-landers will know what ice skating is. Maybe they, too, have experienced this in an indoor arena somewhere, or maybe their backyard pond. But ice cake jumping? I'll bet they've never seen this. Our former Put-in-Bay Mayor, Bernard "Mac" McCann, reminded me of the reason our Island kids began this sport. Since the kids here are often involved in wintertime activities that involve the frozen lake, they need to be taught how to get out of the frigid water if they ever fall in. So, in an effort to teach this skill in a fun way, the sport of ice cake jumping began. Heck, I just thought it was a way for teenagers to pass the time during the winter on Put-in-Bay. The object is to jump to as many cakes as you can without falling in. Like a frog jumping lily pads.

As a young girl, in the late winter, as the ice began to break up in the bay, I would sit on the snow-covered ground near the docks and watch with wonder when my older brother, Davey, and his friends, Eric Booker and Todd Blumensaadt jumped from cake to cake. Many times they would slip and fall in but quickly climb out unharmed. It scared me to death, and so I did not participate in this sport while growing up. Finally, a few years ago, I thought it was time to learn ice cake jumping, and so I did! I think I jumped about three large cakes before returning to the shore to watch the others.

Other experiences, such as four-wheeling across the frozen lake to get to the mainland, may seem unique to some, but to many who live here, it's just a money-saving adventure. One day, while visiting Walleyes on Middle Bass to eat the best tasting garlic-Parmesan wings on the planet, I ran into an old friend, George Danchisen. He had come over to Middle Bass via the ice from Catawba. This was good news because Cliff and I had to leave the island the following day. And, as much as I love to fly with our island pilot, John, I appreciate the extra cash I could be spending at T.J. Maxx instead of on a plane ticket to the mainland.

The next day after school, I ran home and, with a slight Wonder Woman spin, put on my superhero outfit—I mean my floatsuit. A floatsuit is a bright orange Coast Guard approved snowsuit that floats in the water. So, if you go through the ice, you'll pop right up like a fishing bobber. As I donned the suit that could possibly assist in saving my life, I zipped myself in tight and instantly felt much braver. My BFF, Mainland Jen, says I'm crazy to even consider crossing frozen Lake Erie, but I reassure her that my floatsuit will keep me alive long enough to crawl out onto safe ice. I wish I could be Wonder Woman and arrive on the mainland via my very own invisible jet, but a bright green four-wheeler will have to do. I also wish I could *look* like Linda Carter as she sported that Star-Spangled Banner-like outfit, but instead, I show up wearing a bright orange and black suit, with my hair all messed up underneath my helmet.

My entire life, I have experienced and continue to participate in things that may seem odd or intriguing to an outsider looking in. But to me, it's just another day in the life of an Island Girl!

6

WHERE DO YOU LIVE?

WHILE IN FLORIDA ON winter break, I ran into a woman who often visits Put-in-Bay. She asked me one of the questions I am asked most often, "Where on the island do you live?" Sometimes I feel like saying, "What? Do you want to know my social security number, too?" Actually, you caught me. I have responded sarcastically with those exact words, but not that day in Florida. When she asked me that question, I answered honestly. I could sense that she was only curious about my island life and not trying to stalk me or anything. But her question did get me thinking about all the places on the island that I've called home.

The West Shore, East Point, in town, and the inner part of the island: these are just a few of the areas on Put-in-Bay that many of us call home. Some of us live in winterized island homes, staying cozy all year, while others live here only when the ferries run, spending the late spring through early fall in beautiful cottages with unique names. I have lived here year-round for most of my life and, having lived in nine different homes on the island, am sort of an expert about all the island areas. Moving is something I do well! Throughout my life on Put-in-Bay, I have come to love each of the locations I have called home and appreciate the beauty and uniqueness of each one of them.

My mom tells me that during the spring of '73, just before I was born, the water was so high near the Monument that on many days she couldn't get back and forth to our house on East Point. So to play it safe, she stayed on the "other side" in Port Clinton, Ohio, until my birth in late April. [The 24th, to be exact, in case you want to buy me diamonds or send me flowers.] When I was just days old and fresh from Magruder Hospital, my parents moved me to our home with my two older brothers, Troy and Davey. Natalie would arrive three years later. I know, I know—with my youthful looks, it's hard to believe that I am the *older* sister.

We lived in the blue house across the street from "The Cummings Home," known today as the beautiful Victorian house owned by Carol Root. In my East Point neighborhood, the family names at the time were Burgraff, Traverso, Marquard, Crow, and Barnhill. They were always kind to me, even though I was that annoying little neighbor girl who never stopped talking. Three of those families are still living there today. The house that I call my first island home is still blue today and holds my earliest Island Girl memories.

I remember walking down to the Barnhills' beach to swim. I loved the water even then—but not the seaweed. A very young Christie would complain, "I don't like swimming in the grass." The Barnhills also had a daughter whom I would bother endlessly. Mrs. Marquard lived just down the street, and she had a daughter, too! It was a good thing because I was always looking for someone other than my big brothers to play with. Bindy Barnhill and Laura Marquard were probably glad to see us move when we did. I think they had had their fill of me.

When I was six, my family moved to one of the old Parker

houses located in the inner part of the island. It seemed as if our family doubled instantly because now we lived next to the Riddle kids. There were three of us and three of them. Now we could play football, baseball, and ghost in the graveyard! And between the Ontko and Riddle houses lived Chris Likes. He taught us all new "very colorful" vocabulary words. Mrs. Francine Likes was French, and I could listen to her talk forever. That accent was something I wished I had. Mr. Likes was the Ohio Edison man, and I felt safe knowing that during the blizzard of '78, he was the one fixing our electricity.

We had rows and rows of grapevines right next door to my house. Amongst the rows, the neighbor kids and I would play hide and go seek and conceal ourselves after toilet-papering various neighborhood trees. We learned how to eat grapes until our stomachs ached. My hazy childhood memory tells me that grape season went on forever, when in fact, the season only lasted a couple of weeks. The smell of ripening grapes causes me to have flashbacks of riding my bike to school while watching the sun come up over the tall trees surrounding the vineyards.

I rode my bike or walked to school ["uphill in a blizzard both ways"] oftentimes racing P.J. Riddle. He was in my class and was like a brother to me—as if Troy and Davey weren't enough. To get to school, we rode behind Coopers Restaurant (known today as The Goat) through Shady Path on our banana-seat bikes. We wanted to get there early enough to play dodge ball in the schoolyard (which, by the way, kids aren't allowed to do anymore). That area has now been replaced by a library, gym, and extra classrooms. Ahh!...those were the good ol' days...bike rides through the treacherous woods, kids purposely trying to hit each other with balls, and three grades in each elementary classroom!

When I was all grown up, I lived for a short time on the

West Shore. I loved being a "West Shorian." I know, it's not a word, but what else should I call a person who lives there—a West Shore Person? A Resider of the West Shore? So, I will use it, and I did with pride when I lived there with my two daughters, our dog, and a cat. We lived right across from the ramp, or as I like to call it, "sunset ramp." We were West Shorians for all too short a time.

Nearly every summer day, my girls and I would take our dog, Fair, down to the ramp to see the most beautiful reds and oranges as the sun fell into the lake each night. Fair loved to run up and down along the concrete area, chomping at the waves as if they were filled with dog treats. Those large waves would come splashing in as the *Jet Xpress* passed by, and Meredith, being only six at the time, would scream with excitement—and a little bit of apprehension—as she watched from several feet away. Anna was a daring ten-year-old and loved swimming with her raft, allowing the waves to take her in to shore and back out again.

If my dog could speak, I think she would tell me that the West Shore was her favorite place to have lived. Every morning, as I lay in my bed with Fair curled up at my feet, we could hear the seagulls squawking. They would beckon us to go outside and enjoy the lake. In all seasons, it was a beautiful place to live. I can recall feeling the excitement as the ice came in that winter, and I could update people regularly about who was out fishing. For the first time ever, I knew information about the island before my friend Karen Goaziou did! The West Shore has a unique quality to it. There's no place like it on Put-in-Bay.

After that, we all got to experience life on Bayview Avenue with a huge yard and a home chock full of island history. I got the privilege—along with a lot of responsibilities—to live in the old Nissen house behind the place we now call Mossbacks.

As a child, I called it Ted's Tackle Shop, and remember John Nissen sitting on the steps outside, nearly every day. Like Mr. Nissen, I got to be a caretaker, with about two acres to mow and what seemed like miles and miles of gardens to weed. I was never so tan in all my life! The best part of living there was being close to everything: school, store, and the lake. I hardly ever drove my car.

Finally, I have acquired one of the many Parker properties on the island to make my home. It is in the inner part of Put-in-Bay on what many call The Winery Road and is surrounded by quiet woods and wonderful neighbors. Shortly after buying this house, I was told by my Aunt Betty that she and my Uncle Bill were both born here. Just down the street, Joan "Ma" Wertenbach, keeps a watchful eye on not only the neighborhood cats, but also our chickens. One day at school, a student said to me after going home for lunch, "Miss Christie, the cat lady was helping your chickens cross the road." It sounds like a joke, but it wasn't. She really was helping my pet chickens find their way back home. What a great neighbor she is! Another neighbor, John Dodge, takes care of my dog and cat while we're away—and he isn't even a dog lover. Who could ask for better neighbors?

I feel lucky to have experienced life on Put-in-Bay and in so many different locations. We just recently put in a backyard pond. Does this mean I can say I live near the water once again?

One summer night, as Cliff and I were returning home in a taxi filled with about six other adults, I was describing to the driver where I lived. We didn't know each other, so I was directing him. "Turn left at the Winery; then it's the first house on your left past the woods."

He announced, "Oh, I know where that house is—you mean where The Old School Teacher lives!"

Cliff thought this was hilarious. Pointing to me in the cab, he said, "She's right here!" he continued through his laughter, "And, she's not old!"

I did not laugh. I know *funny*, and this was *not* funny! We got out of the cab, and the driver must have seen the shock on my face because his last words were, "It's on me!"

P.S. As many of you may know, my grandfather, Alfred Parker, was commonly known as "The Old Man." But he *was* old. Will people someday pass a house where I had once lived and refer to it as a place where "The Old School Teacher" lived?

Let's hope not.

7

CHARLIE TUNA

WHEN I INTRODUCE MYSELF to people around these parts, they hear my last name and often ask, "Is Charlie Tuna your dad?"

"Yes!" I say with pride.

They beam with excitement as they tell their detailed stories about my dad letting them inside the pilothouse on one of the ferries of which he was captain. He would let them steer the boat or blow the horn as it was coming into the dock. As they talk, I recall my own past. As a young child, I would run up the stairs of the *Yankee Clipper* to the high pilothouse where my dad was captaining the boat. I would sit on top of the tall captain's chair and maneuver her with that giant wooden wheel. Then, when he went to work for Miller Boat Line, I would climb the steel steps to the top of the pilothouse on whatever boat he was manning that day. My dad made me feel so special, and though I always thought I was his favorite, I'm sure he made all the other children feel as special as I did.

My dad grew up in Marblehead, Ohio, another small community on the mainland directly across the lake from our little island. So, you could say I'm half and half—a mutt, really. I am half Islander and half Marblehead girl. My dad's father, "Pa," was born in Margecany, Slovakia, and moved to Marblehead when he was a young man. So, now you know where the name "Ontko" is from. We are not Hawaiian (although, that would be pretty cool), and please don't ask us to speak Japanese. To pronounce this amazing last name, speak it in two syllables. "Ont" rhymes with "font." Now, say the ending "ko." It rhymes with "Joe." You've got it!

My dad is very proud of his heritage. Growing up in our house, my brothers and sister and I knew where we came from. When I was a girl, he would rant in Slovakian, or a "funny dad" made-up version of it. None of us understood the words, but I would mimic him and have so much fun speaking those strange sounds. He always made me feel a sense of pride to be from Slovakia.

I never got to meet my Grandpa Ontko because he died when my dad was only ten, leaving my grandmother to raise twelve children. My Grandma Ontko was a petite little lady full of enough love for all of her grandchildren. The last time I checked, there were 48 of us. She had more patience than anyone I can remember and spoiled us with sweets from her Pinocchio cookie jar.

I got my love of the stage from my dad. He enjoys being the center of attention and making others laugh. When he tells a joke, it may or may not be funny, but what is humorous is just watching him during the telling of the joke. The way he covers his mouth when he chuckles and shakes his entire body—this is the funny part. Many times I have to remind him to keep his jokes politically correct, but I think that's why he tells them to me, for the shock value. I swear, sometimes he is just like one of my students at school.

Whenever and wherever I go with my dad, he will always run into someone he knows. Really, this is true—I'm not exaggerating. With a big smile and an outstretched hand, he will quickly introduce himself to a person he hasn't seen in about 50 years and then start sharing a story with this surprised person about Marblehead, the Army, or his Ferry Boat past. And, if this long lost friend is from anywhere in the Central European area, he/she is instantly one of us—a Slovak. He will proudly show off a little bit of this language as he rattles off a few sayings.

I have learned more from my dad than just how to blow the horn on the ferry or to speak a few words in Slovakian. He has overcome many obstacles in his life that others have never had the courage to face. He has passed this ability and many other qualities onto me. Even though I haven't led a perfect life (show me one person who has), he has always loved me through all my mistakes and lessons. Throughout my life, my dad has shown me that laughter really is the best medicine, and the simple things in life, such as a ride on a ferry boat, are worth more than anything a millionaire can buy.

Please wish my dad, Charlie Tuna, a happy birthday on June 11th. He is turning 70-something, but you would never guess it because of his youthful ways. He continues on to this day, sharing his enthusiasm for life with all of his neighbors on Catawba Island, where he can still hear the Miller Ferry boat horns every day. He lives there with Marcia, his wonderful, loving, and patient wife. I'm sure she still enjoys his fun-loving shenanigans, but I don't blame her if she pushes him out the door when it's time for another card game at the Moose Lodge in Port Clinton. She can only laugh at so many jokes in one day.

8

SMART LINES

A S I GET MY classroom ready for my fifteenth year of teaching, my mind always drifts to past events that occurred in this very same school. I get a little sentimental each time I wander through those hallways. I think of my grandmother, who came over from Middle Bass Island during her high school days. I think of my own mom wearing a poodle skirt to school and of my days as a student there with big 80's hair. Now, I am taking over the classroom of Karen Wilhelm, who just retired, and my mind shifts to more recent events. One memory in particular comes to mind.

I spent my first eleven years as an educator teaching first graders, and during that time, I made it a priority to read a picture book to my students every day. I would settle into my old wooden chair to read. It just so happens, it was the same one Mrs. Goaziou (a.k.a. the Candy Bar Lady) used when I was in her first-grade class about thirty years prior. I would crack open the book of the day and take my students to a magical land, just as Mrs. Goaziou had lovingly done years ago. With even the slightest movement, such as the turning of the pages, that old chair would creak with age. Each day as I sat in the antique chair, I wondered how many stories had been read from it and how much knowledge it had helped to share throughout its many years at Put-in-Bay School.

Although I am not full of ancient wisdom (yet), I have had experiences that others have not, and am always eager to share my knowledge. That day, as I was getting ready to read to my students, I was a little more excited than usual because I was going to read one of my all-time favorite picture books: Tomie DePaola's *Strega Nona*. Suddenly, one of my brightest and most energetic boys interrupted. Normally, an interruption would have been met with a stern look from me and no response, so as not to distract from the brilliant words that flowed from the pages of the daily book. This outburst, however, could not be disregarded.

"Miss Christie, what are all those lines on your forehead?" Robby* asked.

His question was so genuine, as are most questions that bubble up out of a six-year-old's mind. It wasn't as if he were a sarcastic high school kid. However, this all came as little consolation because I didn't know these lines even existed *anywhere* on my face. I thought "lines" were on the faces of the elderly. Was I, like my reading chair, showing signs of age?

"Lines?" I asked with a quiver in my voice. I was obviously shaken by the thought.

"Yeah, those lines. What are they, Miss Christie?" he pressed.

I put the book down gingerly on my lap, and from out of nowhere came my answer, "Well, Robby, those are my smart lines!"

"Smart lines?" he asked, just to make sure he'd heard me correctly.

Then, with almighty teacher wisdom that would make my former principal, Kelly Faris, proud, I continued, "I got those lines from years of growing smarter. I have had two children, and being a mom makes you really smart. And, I have gone to college for many, many years." I took a deep breath and then continued. "I had taught school for years before you were even born! I have read many books and written many stories. I have worked lots of summer jobs all over the island. That's how I got my smart lines, and you will get them someday, too."

I wasn't lying. Really, I wasn't. These lines *were* from all that I've experienced. Don't things we live and feel bring us intelligence that cannot be put into a grade? Being smart doesn't mean just getting all A's or getting a PhD. The proof of all this learning is in the lines on the faces of people everywhere. Getting smart lines just means that I have learned and lived more than someone without those beautiful lines on their face (or that I didn't get Botox).

I was quite proud of myself for the explanation I gave to my students, that day. While basking in my own glory, I looked down at my amazing children. There they were on the carpeted floor listening to me tell them about my smart lines, all the while manipulating their eyes and noses in a failed attempt to make the same contours on their own faces.

The next morning, Robby came running (literally) into the classroom and shouted at me, "Miss Christie, those lines are *not* called smart lines…they're called *wrinkles*. My mom said so!"

Robby isn't this child's real name. I have never taught a Robby in all my years as a teacher, so I thought this a safe name to use.

9

MY MIDDLE BASS PIANO

M Y THIRTEEN-YEAR-OLD DAUGHTER, MEREDITH, has been trying to learn a song on the piano. Every day after school, and sometimes during our crazy lunch hour, I hear the sounds of the instrument made so delicately and precisely by my daughter's steady hands. Then comes the one key near middle "C," the one that is missing its intonation. That ivory rectangle can only create a hollow-sounding thunk.

With a bit of annoyance in her voice, Meredith hollers from the dining room, "Mom, can we get this key fixed?"

"I have. It just doesn't want to stay fixed!" I respond back from the kitchen.

Can I blame our Baldwin Acrosonic upright piano for not being perfect? After all, it has been moved to and from several island homes. It even took a ride on Miller Boat Line to mainland Lakeside, Ohio, where my family lived for several years during the winter. In an attempt to redecorate our house on a budget, my daughters and I have dragged that heavy thing over rugs, carpets, and hardwood floors. The most fascinating fact about this piano's history is that it came across the ice from Middle Bass Island. One cold winter day in 1969, with the help of my friend, Bob Stausmire, and my Grandpa Parker's truck, that piano arrived on Put-in-Bay. So, if the sound isn't quite perfect, or if a key just doesn't want to strike the strings inside, I can hardly blame it. As a matter of fact, because of its special past and unique sound, I love it even more!

The way this piano arrived on Put-in-Bay is like that movie from 1993, entitled simply, *The Piano*. It's an intriguing story where the main character is moved to some remote part of the world with her daughter, and one of the personal items she brings with her is a giant pianoforte. The grandiose instrument arrives by rowboat off a big ship onto the beach. My piano is special, too, like the one in that movie. But instead of coming by open water, as in the theatrical version, my piano has that old movie topped—mine arrived via the frozen waters of Lake Erie. Now, that is cool (no pun intended).

I remember plunking away on its keys when I was a child, just as both of my daughters have done. In my Kuemmel-like stubbornness, I would become so intent on learning a new song that sometimes I would shed a tear out of absolute frustration due to my inability to play it perfectly. Other days, my piano was my best friend, helping my fingers strike the keys as precisely as the sheet music read. On those days, I felt like Mozart as I played the two-handed simplistic song *Swans on the Lake* (my dad decided to rename the over-played song: *Ducks on a Pond*). I would pretend I was in a great big auditorium and people were shouting, "Encore! Encore!" Or, perhaps they were shouting "Ontko! Ontko!"

When I phoned my mom and asked for details about this instrument, she referred to it as her piano, but I call it "My Middle Bass Piano." It was originally a gift to my mom from Mary Waedel, a summer resident of Middle Bass. She was a close friend of my grandmother, born on Middle Bass. Mary was originally from Toledo, Ohio, and according to Sue Duff, she was our Put-in-Bay School secretary for a time. When my mom was attending business school in Toledo, it was Mary who gave her rides to and from the big city each week. She was ever so dear to my family, just as the piano was to my mom in 1969, and still is to me today.

I would say that this island piano and I share many of the same qualities. We have both been daring and fearless, riding across the frozen waters of Lake Erie. We may sound a little off-key to some, but to others, we sound amazing! My daughters, Anna and Meredith, have learned to play both of us very well—and do quite often. Lastly, some have attempted to tune us, but imperfect we remain, making us all the more unique.

10

TIME TO REMINISCE

LOVE TO BAKE COOKIES. I bake them when I'm sad. I bake them when I'm happy. It's sorta like therapy for me. The only trouble is, many weeks during the school season, I feel as if I simply don't have enough time to bake.

So, one day this fall, I was in a rush to catch the last boat to the mainland. It was daylight savings day, actually. The clock said 4:15. The boat was at 5:00. I was rushing around trying to get the house cleaned, clothes packed, and chickens fed before heading over when I looked on the kitchen counter and saw my two sticks of butter.

The butter I was going to bake with that day.

For those of you, like me, who know about baking, we know that in order to get the dough to bake those cookies in just the perfect way, the butter is the key. Butter must be at room temperature—not too cold from the refrigerator, not too hot, like if left too long in the microwave in an attempt to soften it quickly. It must be just room temperature. I'm tellin' you, this is one of the secrets to great cookies.

Another secret is to use just a little bit more brown sugar than white sugar. I prefer organic. And, lastly, please, please use only *pure* vanilla extract.

After all of the ingredients have been placed inside my big metal bowl, I love the stirring part. I get to smell all the ingredients getting mixed together, knowing that soon I will be able to taste the sweetness of it all. What a treat! Finally, the cookies get placed upon the baking sheet—unless I'm making cutout cookies. Ahh!…good ol' fashioned sugar cookies!

This type of cookie reminds me of Christmastime when I was a young Island Girl. Even though my mother tells people that I never paid attention to her, I did. She was the one who taught me how to bake. In fact, it is because of my mom that I have a love of baking inside me.

Right before the holiday season, Parker Boat Line would dry-dock the *Erie Isle* and *Yankee Clipper*, the freight would begin arriving by plane, and my mom would have extra time to spend with my siblings and me. When we baked together, this meant the busy summer season was over, and family time had begun.

So, at holiday time, the cookie cutters would come out of hiding. The old tin cutters with Santa's face, Christmas trees, and candy cane shapes would sit on the counter, awaiting our little hands to press them onto the softened dough. Mom would cover the entire kitchen table with a white dusting of flour before placing the double batch of Great Aunt Teen's sugar cookie recipe onto the floured surface. This was, of course, so the dough wouldn't stick when rolled out.

We were even allowed to make our own creative concoctions with the bit of leftover dough. My mom always encouraged artistic creations, even though it didn't help me much. I would be safe and make the traditional multi-tiered snowman, the best part being that his bottom ball wouldn't bake as thoroughly, leaving a raw dough taste. One of my favorite things about making cookies is that raw cookie dough taste.

But, please don't phone Martha Stewart just yet, because I said I love to bake, not decorate. When those cookies come out of the oven, it's up to someone else to smear them with frosting or take hours to carefully place decorations upon their cooled tops. Decorating is for artistic people, and that I am not.

However, I *am* a person who looks back upon my life with great nostalgia. As I write this, Christmastime is almost here again, and I always think of my mom and my late Great Aunt Christine (Parker) Rudy. They are the women in my life who gave me a wonderful family tradition. I am named after one of them and share her name with great pride.

That fall November day, as I had all these reminiscent thoughts quickly soaring through my head, I was saddened at the thought of having to put my perfectly softened butter back into the refrigerator for another day. Suddenly I looked down at my new iPhone and realized that it was only 3:15, not 4:15, as my unchanged wall clock read. *Whoo-hoo!* Gotta love daylight savings time! An hour was just what I needed that Sunday afternoon to bake a fresh batch of cookies!

"Erie Isle" laid up for the winter, 1964

11

GRANDMA KUEMMEL'S DIARIES

W HEN I WAS A little girl, I would just love rummaging through our big attic. Whether it was a hot summer day or a cool winter evening, that attic held such precious things that the temperature never bothered me as I sat next to boxes of family memories. My favorite box held my great-grandmother Kuemmel's diaries. In those torn, leather-bound books were words I could not read. They were written in an old German dialect. Most of her words were written very clearly, and when I flipped to April 24, 1973, I saw my great-grandmother's words, "Linda had a duaghet [sic] today. Born Christine Lynn."

I continued reading the wonderful words of my grandmother. "Fishing today." She had to write about such things; she was the wife of a fisherman. Living on Middle Bass Island didn't give one much opportunity for a life of riches, but fishes—yes!

It was my great-great-grandmother who inspired me to begin writing at the age of five or six. I attempted to make my own journal. I got two pieces of cardboard, assembled cut-up pieces of paper, and used masking tape to hold it all together.

"Look, Mom! I made a diary just like Grandma Kuemmel's!" I remember saying proudly. She must have seen right then and there that I have nearly no artistic or crafting abilities, as she soon bought me a real diary to write in.

I tried to write in that diary every night. Some nights I would just say, "Oops, I forgot to write today, so I will apologize for that."

Diaries keep track of many things. They can be filled with the temperature and lake conditions, the births of family members, etc. These were the words of my grandmother Kuemmel. My diaries tend to hold thoughts of my own, growing up as an Island Girl, but instead of the water conditions (which I don't pay much attention to), I wrote of my first heartache, and then my second, and my third....

As I grew older and went through adolescence, my diaries grew all too personal. Just ask my teenage daughter. She got her hands on one of my old journals while rummaging through that old attic one day.

But that's another story altogether.

For now, encourage your children to honor their heritage, and if they are writers, compliment them when they choose to keep a journal of any kind.

You never know; maybe your child will become the next writer for the *Gazette*!

My grandmother,
Elizabeth Kuemmel, ca. 1933

12

LEGACY

TRY WRITING YOUR OWN epitaph. I'm serious. This isn't morbid, but instead, a positive exercise on what it is you're striving to be! So far, mine may sound something like this:

> Here lies Christine "Christie" Ontko. She was the partner of Cliff Fulton and the daughter of the famous Captain Charlie Tuna and Midnight Lady, Linda Parker. She, along with an island community, raised her two daughters, Anna and Meredith. It was her hope that her daughters, as well as the students she taught, would become loving, caring, responsible citizens of the planet. She enjoyed writing and wrote often in journals and on her beloved laptop computer. Oh yeah—and she liked to make people laugh.

When I think of what it is I want to leave behind to my daughters, I don't think of just material objects such as my red Chevy Cavalier. Legacy is more than just stuff; it's the mark you leave on this planet, the imprint you leave on others long after you are gone. Lately, I've been thinking a lot about what I will leave behind on Put-in-Bay, and I want it to be something positive.

There are so many islanders who have passed onto the other side who have left their mark on me. It's impossible for me to write about them here, much less remember them all. That would take forever. But each of them has left an imprint on me, and I look to them for inspiration as to what I want to leave behind. For instance, my Great Uncle Joe from Parker's Garage left behind a legacy of kindness and helpfulness. I often think of him when I want to be inspired. He taught my daughter, Anna, how to fly a kite, and she will always remember this.

Merce Traverso left behind warm memories of the nice lady behind the counter at Tony's. She was quiet and reserved but always seemed to care about us kids. She didn't have children of her own, but I like to think the island kids were like hers. I think even when we were teenagers, hanging out shooting pool and playing the jukebox during cold winter nights, she had her eye on us and gave us a safe haven in which to hang out. Each Friday night, we would all meet at Tony's before deciding what we were going to do that night, which many times consisted of drinking Coke and eating candy bars all night with Merce.

Mary Carr, who just recently passed, will not be forgotten in my memory banks. She always wore a smile and thought of all the graduates each year. In 1991, when I graduated from high school, I got a graduation card and was stunned. I didn't know that this lady I saw in church every Sunday even knew who I was! My mom shared with me that she gave every graduate a card, and in fact, had even given her one when she graduated in 1965. This kind gesture all those years ago has inspired me to honor our Put-in-Bay graduates by participating in the Alumni Association.

Mr. and Mrs. Bill Market have left behind a legacy of helpfulness and service to our island community with their ferry boat business, Miller Boat line. I didn't really get to know them as much as I would have liked, but I see the goodness that they had because they passed this onto their children. I enjoy Billy's wonderful pictures on Facebook. Discussions with Julene are filled with laughter and intrigue. Scott's daughter, Gwena, is kind to my daughter, Meredith. All the great qualities in these people were taught to them by their loving parents. What a legacy!

Legacy seems like such a heavy word, but I encourage each of you to think of what it is you want to leave behind for this wonderful little island community. I know none of us is perfect, and we all have made mistakes, but if we could live our lives thinking of what it is we want to share with the world, then I believe we could live much fuller, richer lives each and every moment.

13

COAT, BOOTS, AND A FOUR-WHEELER

I AWOKE ON FRIDAY, JANUARY 13th to wind, snow, and cold, cold, cold. I don't know why this surprised me, but it did. I guess I was living in my *Fantasy Island* world where winter was sunny each day, the birds sang their happy tunes, and my chickens cluck-clucked outside on the green grass. Wait a minute—that *was* my island winter...until the dreadful date of Friday the 13th this past January. And, I have to admit I really liked the mild weather—a bit too much. The Miller boats were running each day, I could leave my house without having to lace up heavy snow boots, and the sun was shining almost every single day, tricking me into thinking it was April.

All I'm seeing now is blowing snow and gray skies. Due to the winter weather, I can't get to the mainland as easily. And I don't like it. I know, I know, I am supposed to be so excited to see the snow, feel the cold and have the lake freeze. As an islander, I'm supposed to be getting my ice shanty ready and sleep in on these cold winter days. However, I don't really like to ice fish, and teachers can't sleep in any time they want.

"Snap out of it!" I scold myself, "It will be spring soon enough. Live in the moment! You're going to miss that beautiful white stuff someday."

[Yea, right….]

For years I fought this cold, gray Ohio season and still do from time to time, as I did on that Friday. However, about seven years ago, I had, as Oprah says, an "Aha Moment." One December evening during the holiday season, I was invited to Annemarie and Craig Eriksen's house for dinner. We got to chatting about the cold, and at that moment I made the decision to enjoy winter. That evening, after dinner, I ordered the warmest winter gear Land's End had on their website. Thank God for the Internet while living on an island! When those items arrived, my winters were changed forever because now I could finally be warm during the coldest months on Put-in-Bay. I'd figured it out: I had to have the right gear.

I felt like someone had been keeping a big secret from me. I didn't know of those warm boots that could keep your toes warm in -35° weather. Nobody told me that the fashionable coat I had been wearing all my life wouldn't really keep me warm, but instead just looked cute on me. And what about my freezing fingers inside my old gloves? Nobody told me about those hand warmers that magically warm when taken out of their little bags. That is, not until that winter where I got the right winter stuff.

So that you don't have to needlessly suffer as I have in the past, I will share with you all my island winter secrets. First, you must get the warmest clothing you can buy. I mean it. Now, I am not a saleswoman, but if I were, I would sell a coat like mine to every person who prefers warm, sunny days. This puffy, down-filled, brown coat nearly hits the ground, covering my legs. When I put it on, I feel as if I'm putting on a sleeping bag, and I probably could actually sleep in it during one of my many camping trips. I don't care if this coat ever goes outta style because it keeps me warm—and when I'm warm, I'm a much happier lady. When I zip myself inside that long winter coat, I feel as if I'm in Hawaii, a place where the sun rarely stops shining. [I don't really feel as if I'm there. I feel like I'm on Put-in-Bay, but the visual just sounded good.]

Second, get yourself a four-wheeler, because if you're going to tough it out here during winter, you gotta have fun. And, a four-wheeler—or as my BF, Cliff, calls it, an ATV—is just that: a lot of fun. Now, if you have this four-wheeler, get a helmet. These things are the best-kept secret! Not only do they keep you safe in case you fall off one of these wonderful ATV machines, but they keep you warm. A must-have!

Next, please, oh please, buy creepers for the bottom of your boots. These little metal spiky things go on the bottom treads so that when you walk on the ice, you won't slip! They're amazing! I can actually take walks outside during the winter in these things without slipping all over the place. Just remember to take them off when walking inside; they don't mix well with recently refurbished solid wood floors.

Lastly, purchase those little hand and feet warmers. Whoever invented these ought to win a Nobel Prize or something. Just buy them, and you'll see what I mean.

So, maybe you enjoy winter. Maybe you're a person like Valerie Mettler, the woman who was my health and gym teacher. She just raves on and on about how wonderful this season is. Even though winter is my least favorite season, I live by the saying, "When you can't beat 'em, join 'em." So, I have chosen to join them and stay warm while doing so.

There is a quote in an issue of *Whole Living* magazine: "Brisk, crisp, invigorating—remember all the positive sides of winter." Well, if they had asked the Island Girl to write a quote about winter, I would have written, "Coat, boots, and a four-wheeler—stay warm and have fun during an island winter."

14

TEST YOUR ISLANDER-NESS

T'S BEEN WHISPERED ABOUT amongst the cottagers, year-rounders, and tourists. At what point exactly does one become a true Islander?

Just what *does* make one an Islander? I have often asked myself this question and have even questioned my own Islander-ness from time to time. My opinion is this: if you can live here all year long and suffer through foggy or stormy weather when there are no flights, no boats, and no milk at the grocery store, then you can call yourself an Islander—or at least a Year-Rounder. Others may disagree with me, using the old rule of thumb, "You aren't an Islander until the last person who remembers you moving here has died."

In order to clear up all this confusion, I have created an assessment for all of you. If you have any trouble with your test or grading, email me (see my contact info in the front of the book), and I will gladly help. No worries, your score and your name will be kept confidential.

Answer the following questions with this point system:

2 = yes
1 = maybe/sometimes
0 = definitely *not*!

I have completed this test myself and written my answers in italics so you can see how it works.

1. Were you born on any of the Lake Erie Islands?
The last child I know of who gets this honor is Crystal Bykowski, so no cheating here. I will know if you have cheated.

   Does Magruder Hospital in Port Clinton count? Nope—0 pts.

2. Do you live here during the winter months? This does **not** mean you stay until the very last boat, go to your home in a warm and sunny climate, and then come back again on the first boat of the season. You have to actually **live** here.

   Secretly, I am extremely jealous of all those smart people who have an island home and one in a sunny climate, and I just recently purchased a mainland home, so I'd better only give myself 1 pt., here.

3. Are you raising a child or two here, or were you raised here as a child?

   Yes—2 pts.

4. Was your mother born on any of the Lake Erie Islands? Give yourself 1 point if you have a mother-in-law from an island.

   Yes, my mom was born here—in the home owned by Mark and Barbi Barnhill—2 pts.

5. Was your father born on any of the Lake Erie Islands? Again, give yourself one point for an in-law.

   No, Marblehead, Ohio—0 pts. Does an ex-in-law count? No…

6. Were either of your maternal grandparents born on a Lake Erie island?

   Yes, both of them—2 pts.

7. Were either of your paternal grandparents born on a Lake Erie Island?

    No, Slovakia—0 pts.

8. Did you graduate from any of the island schools?

    Yes. In 1991—2 pts.

9. Are you happy and content staying on the island throughout the winter months with heaps of snow and lots of ice on the lake?

    Not really...but I make the best of it—1 pt.

10. Do you stay up to date on what's going on? For instance, do you always know when the boats will stop running and begin again in the spring?

    No, I'm always the last to know everything—0 pts.

11. Can you complete many errands while on the mainland for the day? For instance, can you go to at least two different doctors' appointments, shop for groceries, drop the dog off at the vet and pick her up again, run into Wal-Mart for the prescription the doctor has just prescribed, and then finally run through the closest fast-food restaurant for some dinner for the family before making the last boat?

    YES, definitely YES!—2 pts. for me! I'm tired just re-reading that last test question!

12. Have you crossed the ice on a motorized vehicle?

    Yes—2 pts. What fun it is!

13. Do you have a P.O. Box?

    Yes: #507—2 pts.

14. Do you have an island car? Give yourself an extra bonus point if the car sometimes doesn't start.

    Yes, my Chevy Cavalier—2 pts.—no bonus points, because it actually starts.

15. Lastly, while driving a car on the mainland, do you find
    yourself automatically waving to other cars on the high-
    way?

    *I do this all the time! Those mainlanders must wonder
    about me...—2 pts.*

Two bonus points will be given to anyone who has been
on the computer trying to type "Put-in-Bay / putinbay
/ Put in Bay" for accurate delivery of a package. Or, has
been on the phone ordering something and then has gotten into a long discussion about what we do here in the
winter with the person on the other end of the line.

Whoo-hoo! 2 pts. for me!

Two bonus points go to those who can clean fish.

I receive a great big 0 here!

Two bonus points if you know who Frieda is. Or, if you
live on the other Lake Erie Islands, and you shop at your
island store at least twice a week.

Yes—2 pts.

Add up your points to see how your Islander-ness rates below:

30+:SUPER DUPER AMAZING TRUE BLOODED ISLANDER!
You are able to predict when the ice will come in
just by smelling the winter air. With your family at
the dinner table, you excitedly announce the birth
of a new island baby and, if asked, can draw this
new child's family tree perfectly. Everyone knows
you and your island car. Hopefully, your bloodline
will continue on.

27-29:   A PRETTY GOOD ISLANDER
You probably know the boat schedules relatively
well and can be like a superhero during a trip to the
mainland. You run into the same island folk each
day during your daily trip to the store and post office.
Excellent job being an islander!

24-26   SORT OF AN ISLANDER
You know how to shop on the mainland and probably have an island car that needs to be jump started from time to time, but because of other issues, you cannot be called a real, true islander. It's okay, though. Maybe you can learn to clean fish to up your score.

21-23:   MEDIOCRE ISLANDER
Maybe your island car isn't a beat-up old car that needs an oil change desperately. To get a higher score, have a package successfully mailed to an island. Start listening to what's going on around town. Marry a **SUPER DUPER AMAZING TRUE BLOODED ISLANDER.**

18-20:   ISLANDER IN TRAINING
Are you the first one in your family to live here during the winter? I understand that you may have issues out of your control. If you work really hard, maybe your great-grandchildren can earn a score of 30.

0-17:   ISLANDER WANNABE
Wow…you have lots to do. Get a junky old car, and start waving to everyone! Please talk to J.R. or Margie immediately about getting a P.O. Box. Perhaps you should think about forging some documents to say your family is really from one of the Lake Erie Islands. Lastly, staying here during the winter months and venturing out on the ice will up your score immediately. Gather some fish and go clean 'em. I have faith that you can earn a higher score.

My score was only 24. Thank goodness for those bonus points! I should take lessons from my mom…or anyone in the Schneider family.

Maybe I should rename my column "Sort of an Island Girl."

15

JUST GO FOR A RIDE

GOT INTO MY CAR and turned on the radio.

Silence…again.

This was the fifth day of no sound on my car radio. [You'd think I'd remember after day one.] Of course there's nothing! I left my lights on one foggy morning at school and ran the battery dead, and it—along with the clock—cannot be reset without a special code. My sister sold me the car, and she now lives in Germany. No luck finding the little card with the secret code written on it.

"Why must I have the radio playing on my island car when going about a half-mile down the street?" you might ask. I asked myself this same question that sunny spring day as I was on my usual race towards home. Distraction, I suppose. A mental break from the day.

At home, my busy life awaited me that day as every day does after the school bell rings: the dog, cat, and chickens were hungry; four days of laundry sat inside the hamper not getting any cleaner, and my floors needed washing. Also, my business needed tending to. I would have to find time to look at my website and remind all my girlfriends on Facebook to come to the Open House in May. I am a busy island girl!

As I drove toward home, I decided that instead of turning right, I would continue on past. Even though my time was extra short that day, something told me that I needed to slow down and take a breather. I needed to take in the silence and just go for a ride like I used to do with my parents when I was a little girl.

I quickly forgot all my stresses of the day, driving along the roads of our island, and I thought back to the times of my childhood when one of my parents would say, "Let's go for a ride!" All three of us kids would eagerly pile in the car because we knew it was time to enjoy the island in our own way. When I was a little girl, we never turned on the car radio. We would never dream of it. The purpose was to slowly drive around, enjoying the island, not to listen to music. Those old island cars were the best!

My mom, Linda Parker, owned a two-door 1953 Chevy. To get to the back seat, the front seats flopped over and I could easily crawl inside. I would play with the metal ashtray and loved that metal-on-metal sound as I clicked it open, then closed, then open again. When lucky enough to sit in the front seat, I would play with the push button for the glove box and feel the heaviness of its tiny door when it flopped open with a loud "thud!"

To describe my dad's car is difficult because you'd just have to see it for yourself. My dad, Charlie Ontko, had a car that was a two-toned green 1949 Plymouth. The green colors on top and on the bottom were vibrant and rich. It was just one-of-a-kind, like my dad. When he opened the vent on the hood of the car to let fresh air inside while driving, I thought that was the air conditioning. What a car that was!

Davey, Natalie, and I would play a game when we were on those island rides with our mom. She would hold her cigarette in one hand, and with the other, drive her Chevy with its great big steering wheel. The object of our game was to be able to call out where we were after a few minutes of driving around, our eyes tightly shut the entire time. My sister, brother, and I would crouch down in the back seat so as to ensure that no cheating occurred while quietly listening for any hints. Those moments while we were silent probably gave my mom some much-needed peace and quiet.

Our game sounded something like this:

"Okay…where are we now?" Mom suddenly asked.

"Near the Monument!" I shouted.

"No," Davey interjected, "closer to the Dairy Queen."

My sister, a bit too young to know yet, agreed with big brother Davey. "Yup, near the Dairy Queen!"

"Heads up!" Mom called. Sure enough, we could see we were between the Dairy Queen and the Monument.

All of us kids were experts at this game. We knew the island well and could probably still beat anyone at it today.

My mom was notorious for taking us to see the sunset. Sometimes we would bring along Linda Mahony and her daughters, Karen and Amanda Goaziou. It was our girl time! All four daughters fit snugly in the backseat of the Chevy while Mom and her friend gossiped upfront. It was an unspoken rule that when the sun went down, all chatter would end and we would silently watch the sun fall into the lake.

My dad enjoyed his silence in a different way. He would play a "trick" on us while driving us home in his car. We would head up past Cooper's hill, turn right onto Mitchell Road, and suddenly he would turn off the ignition at the top of the hill. He would take one last puff of his cigarette and let the car quietly coast the rest of the way home. I used to think this was the neatest thing ever—to hear only the hum of the tires on the road and no motor! [Maybe it was my dad's way to save on gas.]

He was very proud of his '49 Plymouth and enjoyed driving through town showing off its new paint job during the busy summer season. I sat in the front seat with him and hung my little elbow out the passenger side window. I felt so special riding around in my dad's island car while watching the tourists roam everywhere.

One time, I recall a boater in cut-off jeans flashing his wallet at my dad as we were driving by. "How much?" shouted the boater.

"Not for sale!" my dad proudly announced. We continued on down the street, and I was on top of the world!

Like those moments of peace during rides around the island as a young child, the silence was there for me during my ride home from school that day. It lasted only about fifteen minutes, but it was just enough time to allow me to pull into my driveway, feeling as if I were young Christie all over again. My peaceful island ride had left me feeling like a million bucks.

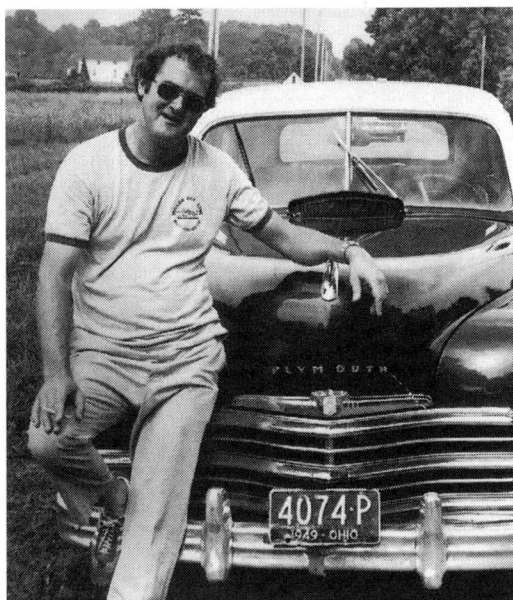

My dad in his "glory days"

16

THE FERRY RIDE

S A FIFTH-GENERATION ISLAND girl of Put-in-Bay, there have been many hours spent out on the lake because my father and grandfather were both ferryboat captains. When I was younger, the coldest, most treacherous outings to the mainland for orthodontist appointments and grocery shopping were taken in the spring and fall. But my most memorable rides were the ones where seagulls would tag along the back of the boat, hoping for a fish or a morsel of the stale bread we would toss out to them. The summertime ferry rides were—and still are a special little secret that I enjoy out on Lake Erie.

There is just something so meditative about the 20 minutes I spend riding that great big ship filled with cars, tourists, and islanders like myself. I sit outside in the back of the boat and relish those precious moments. Where else could I be and not be interrupted by dirty laundry, problems of my teen daughters, and my bills?

The sunshine on my face warms me just enough, while the gentle breeze cools me all at the same time. The sounds of those seagulls are still there, but I know better now. No stale bread—not good for their stomachs. Instead, I encourage them to find a walleye or perch in the water that's been stirred up by the giant propeller of the ferry.

From up top, as I look over the steel railing, I quickly become mesmerized by the water below. The way it changes color and shape with each gentle movement of the vessel always puts in me into a trance. My thoughts often drift to my childhood moments as a young girl. I was so proud of both my father and grandfather and how they protected their passengers each day during those many years at the helm. Other times, my mind likes to take me to faraway places. "Could this boat take me there?" I ask myself in silence.

The ferry ride is sometimes seen as simple transportation to and from the mainland, where many errands often await an Island Girl. The tourists regard it as a new experience and the only way to get to their vacation. Lately, however, and more than ever before, I am enjoying the gift it gives me with each passing of the channel: time to myself.

Mom and Aunt Jeanette on the bow of "Erie Isle"

17

MY GRANDMOTHER'S RING

THIS PAST CHRISTMAS, MY mom bestowed upon me my grandmother's wedding ring. Grandma Elizabeth (Kuemmel) Parker was born on Middle Bass Island to Anna Kuemmel, who was originally from Germany. The ring is a simple gold band with several small diamonds, but you would have thought that Mom had just given me the Holy Grail.

My grandmother died when I was only three, and I was always a bit melancholy because I never really got the chance to know her. I do, however, have faint memories of her. Once, I recall being at her kitchen table eating cereal, and she was telling me not to waste the milk at the end. I remember my belly being full but having to drink every last drop of sugary milk leftover from my cereal because my grandmother had told me to. Even then, I knew never to mess with a strong German woman. My other vivid memory is of her funeral; everyone around me was sad, my mom was crying, and I didn't understand why.

If her ring could hold memories, it would hold such events as the birth of her four children, and after that, the taking care of those little babies. The ring could describe her waking up during the night for 2 a.m. feedings. It would talk about Betty, Bill, Jeanette, and my mom, Linda, being young children. The rebellious teen years would come next, with stories of them staying out past curfew, and then their high school graduations. That gold and diamond band could tell us about the years when my Grandpa Alfred worked hard in the vineyards and then started his own ferryboat business. It would talk of their four children working long hours at Parker Boat Line. It was my grandmother who supported Grandpa and the family through all of those times.

Even though I hardly knew my grandmother, Elizabeth, I see and feel her amongst my family. She is there in my own mother when her sensitive side comes out. My Aunt Betty has her strength. I can see her love in Aunt Jeanette when she comes to school to pick up her grandson, Geoffrey. Uncle Bill has her eyes. And now her name continues on in my own daughter's middle name.

Elizabeth Kuemmel Parker didn't realize the legacy she would leave on this little island of Put-in-Bay. She never dreamt that I, one of her granddaughters who barely had time to get to know her, would carry on the family memories in stories such as these. Did she realize the impact that she would have all those years ago? Did she ever think about her granddaughters having daughters?

I had never realized how much a mother does until my own daughter was born. In the middle of the night, one evening nearly 18 years ago when Anna was a newborn, it was my mom who helped me feed, change, and put her back to sleep. It was in that early morning that I realized that Mom had done this for me, too, when I was a newborn, as had her mother before her. My thoughts had never gone there before. Selfish. That's what I had been in my teens and early adulthood. But then, as a new mother, things had changed instantly.

I wonder if my grandmother, Elizabeth, ever realized how

much my mom would go on to teach me and how I would enlighten my daughters. This past Christmas, I felt as if my mother had knighted me—that I had finally earned the right to wear my Grandma's beloved wedding ring. Or, maybe my mom was finally ready to part with such a precious piece of her own mother. Whatever the thought behind the gift was, I am grateful to my mom for giving me that ring and for so much more.

Spring always brings work and activity to our islands, and we can become wrapped up in our own lives. I share this story in hopes that in the midst of your busy day, you will remember to say, "Thank you" to the hundreds of moms who got up in the middle of the night, survived teenage years, and continue to support and love their children well beyond the age of 18.

Happy Mother's Day to all our island moms!

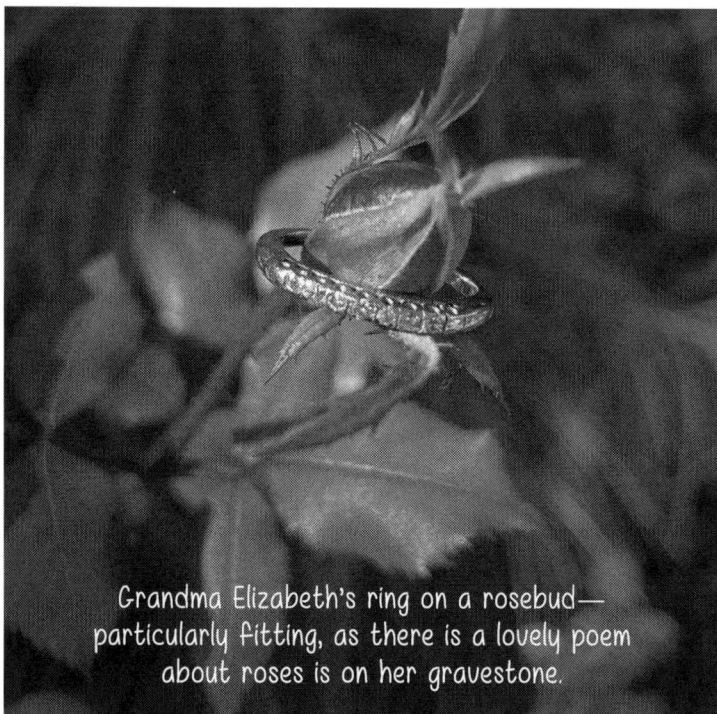

Grandma Elizabeth's ring on a rosebud— particularly fitting, as there is a lovely poem about roses is on her gravestone.

18

AN ISLAND GRADUATION

S OON, I WILL WATCH as my oldest daughter, Anna Elizabeth Engel, receives her Put-in-Bay High School diploma. As the tears begin to well up in my eyes, that day, what will I be thinking, feeling, and seeing? Maybe I won't cry at all. Maybe I will be filled with so much pride that it will bubble up from inside and come out through my beaming smile! Possible thoughts of regret may also be felt. "She can't leave me, yet! I haven't taught her enough for her to be out in the *real world!*" Or, will I be concerned about any last minute details of the graduation party at the Yacht Club afterward? Hopefully, through all my thoughts and emotions that day, I will have time to see and thank all in this community who have helped my daughter throughout her years of life.

Along with her on the stage on June 8th, will be Miranda Krueger and Dallas Mohn. On that day, I will also see my youngest daughter, Meredith, receive her 8th grade diploma, followed by Jessica Krueger and Ian Pippert-Ladd. These children have all passed through my classroom when they were first graders and now, all these years later, I will be there with them to celebrate this transition into the next phase of their lives. Each year, Put-in-Bay School holds its graduation, and many of the islanders are there, along with family, teachers, and friends supporting these kids, now all "grown up." With the love and support of this island community, these children have made it!

My mom will be at the ceremony, as she is almost every year. Sitting beside me, I wonder what her thoughts will be. Maybe she will be reliving her own Put-in-Bay graduation of 1965, or possibly she may be thinking about her mother, who also graduated from Put-in-Bay School with a diploma in 1931. Many other island families have had multiple generations of graduates, as well—the McCanns, Foxes, Dresses, and Heinemans, just to name a few. All of these families have been helped by our school and have learned lessons from this community that couldn't be found in any textbook (or even in today's school—the Internet!).

Our island graduation didn't seem that unique to me, back in 1991. Yes, I knew that my class was small: only 5, compared to my friend Mainland Jen's class of 45 or so, and the numbers don't even compare to my summer friend, Berni Isaly. She was from Westlake, Ohio, and her class had at least 200 in it! I didn't realize back then just how special that day long ago would be to me, someday. I didn't think of myself twenty-one years later at my own daughter's ceremony.

It will be slightly different, but at the same time, full of tradition that we islanders treasure so much. For many years, the ceremony was held at the Town Hall, and then in 1973, it was moved to the Peace Memorial, the structure known to us simply as "The Monument." No longer are we allowed to hold the actual ceremony beneath the great granite column. Now we hold it on the platform of the amazing visitor's center, where the audience can behold the Peace Memorial in the reflection of the tall glass windows. If it rains, the students will be on the new stage at the school auditorium, the same building that was under construction the year I graduated. After the diplomas have been handed out and the usual "Seize the Day!" speeches have been made, the new graduates, islanders, family, and friends will walk or take the short drive to the Yacht Club.

The next night, those same high school graduates will be inducted into the Put-in-Bay Alumni Association, where they will be forced to sit through a long dinner while listening to speeches given by former graduates. As the honored guests, these new graduates will get a fabulous free meal! They will hear colorful stories from 25 and 50 years ago. They will honor past graduates and bow their heads in remembrance of those no longer with us. Those three young adults will sit together at a table, and two of them will notice family members at the banquet, too. Dallas Mohn will see his mom, a 1983 Put-in-Bay graduate. As for my daughter, Anna, she will have both her parents in attendance, as well as her maternal grandmother. This annual Alumni Banquet is not only special and unique, compared to other school reunions, but each year I enjoy the opportunity it gives me to reminisce and laugh about those times years ago.

In June of 1991, I had just turned eighteen and was already living on my own in Boardwalk Housing (because, of course, I knew it all and wanted to be independent and do my own thing). On the day of my graduation, the weather couldn't have been more perfect. The *Sonny-S* blew its horn long and loud, in a rebellious-high-school sort of way. It was a way to celebrate the graduates...and it also interrupted the speaker. It made me laugh, which is just what I needed to help calm my nerves. I had to make a speech and my sister and I had to sing a duet in front of everyone! [I actually sang—in front of *people*!] Lastly, I remember feeling so excited and that I wanted to get *outta* there, get to the Yacht Club, and party with my fellow graduates.

The five of us had agreed to stay up all night and then go together for breakfast the next day. I got the idea from my mom. Back in 1965, her classmates had fun together the night of their graduation and then met the next morning at the Log Cabin. This was one of the island's favorite restaurants once located across the street from Fox's Dock, and owned by Cherrie Galvin's family, who was also a 1965 graduate. The Snack House was our breakfast destination, and I confirmed with Kristin Altoff, the other girl in my class, that four out of the five of us 1991 graduates had made it to our breakfast that next morning.

What will my daughter and her classmates do? They probably have their own ideas of how to celebrate their commencement. The plan is to head to the yacht club, where they will hold the annual graduation party, celebrating with the entire community. This is a tradition I am glad to see continue. I have no idea what they are going to do afterward. Since there are only three of them, they may all go their separate ways to entertain out-of-town guests. Maybe they will pull an all-nighter as former graduates have done before them, and then eat breakfast early the next morning at Pasquales or Frosty's. Will they be filled with gratitude when all is said and done and their parties are over?

To be honest, my thoughts during that time in 1991 focused on my feelings of celebration, and I'm sure this is universal to graduates all across the U.S.A. However, I do remember being so thankful for the scholarships I received, along with the cards and gifts from everyone; it was a bit overwhelming. Upon receiving my scholarships at graduation, both my mom and dad breathed sighs of relief that were probably audible to those in the chairs that day. I had a savings account filled with cash from summer jobs, first communion money, and some savings bonds that my parents had purchased. But even with those scholarships and my savings, I knew that it would take many more days of working during the summer and on weekends in order for that bursar bill at Bowling Green State University to get paid. It's because of the support of this island community and my family that I was able to receive my degrees, come back here to teach, and raise two daughters.

The well-known African proverb could be rephrased to read "It takes an island to raise a child." On our island of Put-in-Bay, it proves itself time and again, and I see it on a daily basis at school. Like my mother and grandmother before me, this island community was there for me that day in 1991 and will now be there on June 8th to support my daughter, Anna. Will she someday come back to live here and help our community as it has helped her? Will Dallas and Miranda have grandchildren that will someday look back upon generations of family members who have graduated from this little island school? We will have to see. But whatever the future holds, I hope that these three graduates hold the feelings of gratitude and loving memories of Put-in-Bay wherever life takes them. I certainly do—and life took me only about a mile down the road.

Christie (the author) Meredith, Linda (Mom & Grandma Parker) and Anna, the graduate

19

DREAMING

ERE I AM AT the beautiful State Park beach on a glorious summer day. I have the day off because I teach right here in our wonderful Put-in-Bay School and have chosen for about three years now not to take on a summer job. This particular summer, I opted not to take any classes, either. Instead, I am spending time with my family, writing, and enjoying the lake. Today we are watching the graceful sailboats passing by. Cliff and I dream of someday owning one of those boats and living very simply. Having only what we need. Using solar and wind power to generate enough power for our onboard refrigerator. Live on the water and catch our perch dinners each night. What a great life! But there is one big problem—I don't know how to sail.

Even though this silly little obstacle exists, I can still see Cliff and me sailing through calm waters, sipping our fancy drinks, and watching each and every sunset. I will be wearing some cute little white outfit with a visor on my head in order to keep the reflection of the hot summer sun to a minimum. Ahh!…that's the life! We will sell all our worldly possessions, giving all the proceeds to The Historical Society (of course), and move onto that tiny little boat. Except…I can't get rid of my book collection...or my shoes. I have to have books to read while on board, after all, and I need my shoes to protect me from the sun on the hot deck—right? Maybe we'll have to buy a pretty large boat with an extra big closet.

I've actually never even been sailing. Now, you're probably shocked. You're probably wondering, "Why doesn't a fifth-generation Island Girl know how to sail? Why hasn't she ever been sailing? This amazing lake is all around her!"

Cliff has an excuse for not knowing how to sail: he was born on the mainland and stayed there for a large portion of his life. He lived in suburban America. When he wasn't at the fair with his daughters or watching his son play football, he was traveling the world with his job. Now that he is a year-round island guy, however, he is falling in love with the water more and more each day and wants to be out on the lake as much as possible.

Instead of learning how to sail as a teenager, I chose the route of working. Like many island kids, life on the island consisted of a summer job. I thought about it all winter. "Where can I work and have fun? Where can I make the most money?" I liked working and making new summer friends. I had my own money with which I bought my first ten-speed bike. But most of my money was carefully put in my savings account for college so that I could earn the teaching degree I dreamed about. So, learning to sail, I did not. Saving money and making friends, I did.

I'll try to help you understand a little bit more about my Island Girl life. As a teenager, I was so busy keeping the island alive with service to our tourists during the summer months that I simply didn't have time for a leisurely boat ride to other islands or even a serene sail on the lake at sunset. An occasional ride on a friend's powerboat across the lake in the fall or early spring due to the shortened ferry schedules, maybe.

But, joy rides? It just didn't happen.

Another reason I never learned to sail is that it scared me to death. In order to take sailing lessons, I had to tread water for like an hour or something. I also remember being told that I would have to get up really early in the morning during the *summer*! Do you know a teenager who actually enjoys getting up before 8 a.m. in the summertime? I didn't think so. And those sails that you have to crank up and down depending on wind conditions—another very frightening thought. I would have to learn how to read the wind, *then* have to watch my head as that big stick thing that is attached to the sail comes swinging around the boat. I could have died while taking sailing lessons.

And did I mention I get seasick? Just ask anyone who has ever ridden Miller Ferry with me, even on a *slightly* windy day. If you are the poor soul who happens to be sitting in "my" seat, the one seat on the boat that prevents me from spilling my supper all over the place, then watch out. If you're in that seat, I will practically push you overboard so I can sit there. You see, there's a place on those big boats that is the least movable during stormy weather so that the effects of the boat's motion are much less. I don't have special non-seasickness powers just because I'm an Island Girl, no matter what you all may think.

Maybe I just wasn't meant to be a boat person. Please don't ask me to use fancy vocabulary words. I hear boat people saying such things as "starboard, port, bow, and stern." I just say "right, left, front, and back." Do I really have to use directional words such as east and west? The other day while riding aboard my brother Troy's boat, I heard myself say, "Go to the right side of Middle Bass! Over there!" He knew what I meant. However, my deceased grandpa, Captain Alfred Parker, would not be pleased with me. I obviously never paid attention as a child while riding on his ferry boat. I must have been too busy eating the ice cream cone he bought for me during our stop at Middle Bass. Or, upchucking that very same ice cream into a five-gallon bucket on the back of the boat on the way home.

I have it all figured out! After Cliff and I retire, we'll sell all our worldly possessions (but keep my shoes), buy me some cute sailing outfits, and get that magnificent sailboat. Instead of taking all the time to actually learn those words and figure out wind conditions, we could hire an experienced sailor, and he can do all the work for us! Now, doesn't this sound like the way to do it? But each time I speak of this, Cliff quickly reminds me of my seasickness. For now, we will continue to dream... and stock up on Dramamine.

20

THE KOOL-AID STAND

T.J. (Tyrus) Burgess and I grew up together. Both of us were island kids, and our moms were friends, having gone to school together on Put-in-Bay. His oldest sister, Tracy, babysat for us Ontko kids. I can remember putting on plays for our parents, peddling the old metal cars in the back of his house on the concrete slab, and petting his goat that lived in the back near the chickens. But in my opinion, the most important thing that T.J. and I did together as young kids was to set up our weekly Kool-Aid stands.

Being in sales was something that came naturally to us. After all, we were among the tourists every day on Put-in-Bay, and we had to cash in on some of it, right? So, we would plan. During the week, we would think about what the weather was going to be like for the upcoming weekend because, of course, there were more tourists during the weekends. We would make our signs. We would buy the Kool-Aid and cups (or "borrow" them from our moms' cupboards). Ice would be made daily and stored in bowls inside the freezers at both houses. We were serious about our Kool-Aid.

In the morning, we would set up the stand, most of the time in front of T.J.'s busy street: Airport Road. That's where the most tourists would bike or walk by. Sometimes we would set up at my house on Mitchell Road, but it was more of a moneymaker if we did it at his house. Plus, to me, my house was boring. His was full of wonderment. He had toys that I didn't have. Cats were everywhere, and I love cats! And, he had those cool chickens and a goat.

We had a strategy to our selling. We were big on making cardboard signs that clearly stated the service we were offering, and to target our audience, we put them along Airport Road on the telephone poles. Arrows were also placed upon the signs, colored in with dark black permanent marker (the kind that smelled good to you when you were a kid and are practically illegal to use in schools today).

There was another kid down the street who used to sell Kool-Aid, too. He was a summer kid. We didn't like him. He was our competition, our rival, "The Mystery Kool-Aid Kid." One of our strategies, besides selling the best Kool-Aid ever, was to outsmart him with those great signs we made. We hoped that the tourists would bypass his stand and only come to ours. This was serious stuff!

We would ride our bikes down to check out his stand. There he would be, behind the small table that he had set up, selling *his* Kool-Aid. Maybe he even dared to sell Lemonade? We would never know this information and couldn't meander too long because we didn't want him to know that we were actually spies—the kids from down the street with the other stand. We found out many years later, that "The Mystery Kool-Aid Kid" was Mikey Chervenak. I wonder if he ever knew of the serious competition we gave him. Maybe he will now.

Besides creating signs, careful preparation, and having the best location, we had the most effective strategy of all: we put my little sister, Natalie, outside at our stand. She was cute…

and, I mean *cute*. She was blonde with big dimples and smiled all the time. We used her cuteness to lure those tourists to our stand. And it worked!

T.J. and I would sit inside his bedroom and watch out the window as Natalie made sale after sale. The tourists would even tip her! Boy, was she good! When we discovered this tactic, it added greatly to our daily income and made our days selling Kool-Aid much easier (for T.J. and me). While Natalie sat outside selling, we would sit inside or play in the yard. We still kept a watchful eye on my little sister at our Kool-Aid stand, though. When it came time to stirring up another batch or bringing out more ice, we were on the ball.

Natalie didn't seem to mind sitting out there selling our Kool-Aid. She seemed to like it, actually. The best part about little Natalie being our bait was that she didn't know much about money. We paid her in Kool-Aid.

I'm not sure if our parents ever knew of our deep love of our Kool-Aid Enterprise, nor do I know if they knew about us making Natalie sit out there. Those long, hot days selling that stuff near the road taught us island kids so many things, such as how to be resourceful, work together, and make money. But I think the most important lesson that we gained from it all was when put to good use, little sisters can be good for something.

21

YELLOW, BLUE, RED, AND GREEN

CLIFF AND I DECIDED to meet up with Libby and David Miller and their family out on the lake, one sunny day in August. Summer is always a good time to catch up with my childhood friends who have moved away. As we set our anchor into the sandy bottom of Schoolhouse Bay, I noticed that Chris Miller was already wading in the waters of Lake Erie, and three of Libby's kids were swimming happily. Cliff and I got out of our boat to talk and have a cocktail, all while feeling that sandy bottom beneath our feet. In that afternoon conversation, we reminisced about our softball days of the 70's and 80's on Put-in-Bay.

Much like today, it was the most important thing to many a kid during summers on the islands. This sport gave the summer kids and year-round kids alike a reason to get together in camaraderie and also experience some great competition amongst the four island teams. The Little League program was very well organized, and we have our parents, coaches, and numerous other volunteers, to thank for that. With mixed ages of 6–12, children would play ball together, with the older kids eager to help the younger ones.

I have a memory of my first season on the Yellow team. I

was rounding the bases and heading home—probably after Eric Turner had hit yet another amazing home run! We were on the old field behind the school, where the gymnasium is now, and I was just learning how to play. David Banta, who was a few years older than I, was on my team and cheered me on the whole way around the bases.

"Come on, Christie!" he called as my little legs took me past third base. "Run!"

I looked up and saw that Banta boy hollering my name, and he gave me just the encouragement I needed to get across the plate. Unfortunately, my approach to home plate was "somehow interfered with"—I think I tripped over a bat (or, at least that's what I tell myself). I totally wiped out, skinning my elbows and covering my brand new jeans with the dusty dirt that surrounds every home plate. It was David Banta who picked me up, put me on his shoulders, and paraded me around the protective fencing behind the field. Through my six-year-old tears, my embarrassment quickly left me, and all I felt was pride, which I can still feel today, 33 years later. David remained on the Yellow team with me until his family moved off the island to Nebraska.

Ahh!…the Yellow team! We began like The Bad News Bears—never winning, but as the years progressed, we got good and actually won a championship or two! But to be fair, I must mention the other three teams: Blue, Red, and Green. If you research color meaning, you will find that yellow means cheeriness, happiness, and action. Blue is said to mean truth, healing, and tranquility. Optimistic, dynamic, and intense are represented by the color red. Green signifies nature, generosity, and success. Ask anyone between the ages of 35 and 45 from Put-in-Bay what color team they were on, and they will quickly tell you (maybe their personalities match their old team color?).

When discussing the Put-in-Bay Little League of long ago,

the conversation still gets a little competitive. "The Mean Green Machine team was the *best!*" David Miller boasted as he handed me a cocktail that day in the water.

I shot back, "Don't forget, the Yellow team had Eric Turner, and he could hit a home run nearly every time on that old field!"

Libby and David Miller were on the "Mean Green Machine" team, along with all three of the Riddle family kids. And they *were* mean (not really, but they tried to act that way so they could win the championship). Libby and David have a picture of each of them individually in their green shirts, holding their bats, just under a photo of the entire team, all matted, framed, and hanging proudly on their wall. They remember this time fondly as they began their friendship then, and now all these years later can proudly say that they have been married for 14 years.

If my memory serves me correctly, Megan Faris was on the Red team. The Cooper Boys, Jason and Chris, along with Berni Isaly and Jill Turner, were all Yellow team players. Robin Burris informed me she was on the North Bass Island team (I don't recall that team color—sorry). Tommy Dailey was a member of the Blue team but recalls being more comfortable with a guitar in his hands rather than a baseball bat. Still, if you ask him today what year the Blue team won the championship game, he will quickly tell you, "1981."

In a recent text, T.J. Burgess filled me in on his family. He and his sister, Tanya, were on the Blue and Green teams, respectively, and T.J. even played on the Yellow team with me for a while.

"Eventually, I just gave up" is what T.J.'s last text message read. Like T.J., I felt like giving up after my first year. Quite frankly, I didn't know what I was to do when I first started my six-year stint as a Yellow team player. My coaches, Scott Parker and Boo Prendergast put me in right field. That's because nobody ever hit balls out there, and all the newbies had to play that position. I recall sitting down out in the field because I was bored—not to mention *hot!* [Sitting down would make the time go faster and also cool me down—right?] But I was quickly spotted sitting down out there, in my extra-big yellow shirt (they didn't have small sizes then). My caring coaches told me I could *not* sit down in the outfield. Actually, I think Scott, who was also my cousin, yelled at me, "Christie, STAND UP!"

After my first season of not knowing what to do, I was determined to get better and become part of the action. My brother, Davey, would help prepare me in our yard each spring and as long into the fall as the weather would allow. He would hit balls to me, and many times the Riddle kids would join us, too. Of course, our little sister, Natalie, was also in training. Grounders, fly balls, and line drives, too—Davey would remind me to use both hands as I caught the ball. He was patient with me and tough on me at the same time.

After a few more years of softball playing, I was determined to become a pitcher. Brandi Walton was a Yellow team pitcher, and being a few years older, I knew her time was running out. So, after a few tries at second and third bases, I knew I wanted more. I asked Davey to now help me learn to pitch. It was something I had to work toward, and work I did!

I summoned my courage and asked my coaches if I could try pitching, and they said, "YES!"

Whoo-hoo! My summertime Little League career as a pitcher had begun! I remember the pressure was high, but I loved it. As a pitcher, I was involved in every single play. If I didn't pitch well, then the plays couldn't even begin. There was a lot of pressure, but it was filled with excitement at the same time. I would actually cry after a game if I hadn't pitched my best. [Don't tell my brother, he would *totally* make fun of me.] I would head out to the mound each game and feel more alive than ever, with serious ten-year-old competition running through my veins.

It also brought the competitive spirit out in the parents. David Miller recalls that green shirts were made saying "Mean Green Machine." His mom, Reni Miller, along with Sue Amrine, proudly wore those green shirts as they cheered on their kids. My parents would make it when they could, and the bleachers would really fill up during the championship game.

As we all waded in the water at Schoolhouse Bay that hot summer day, the talk of softball brought us back to an easier time in our lives and brought out the young kid in each of us. Even to this day, the friendly competition could still be felt. Playing softball brought all of us island kids together each and every summer, all those years ago, and it did the same on that August day on the lake. It is a tradition this island will continue to treasure for as long as there is summertime. It even brought two ballplayers together in marriage!

22

DON'T YOU DARE!

THIS ISLAND HOLDS WHAT I call "the family rule." I can complain for hours about my family. I can whine about my nosy mom and how she always knew about the trouble I got into while growing up. [Good job, mom!] I am allowed to comment on the life of my Grandpa Parker and his stubborn, tough behavior. Or, I can complain about my teenage daughter, Anna.

But, don't you *dare* talk badly about my family!

The island is like that to me. I can say things about Put-in-Bay like, "Ugh! The winter is so cold and long...no boats...no T.J. Maxx." Or during the summer months, "Those annoying tourists took up every spot in the grocery store parking lot—again!"

But don't *you* talk badly about the island. Don't you *dare* call my Island "Pick-up-Bay!"

Yes. You read that correctly.

A few years ago, I was in Yellow Springs, one of my favorite Ohio towns. It's several hours south of here, and it's oh-so-cute with a neat little college called Antioch. I was meandering through its streets on an early morning walk in April, when I noticed a woman about my age tending to her garden. I stopped to comment on how lovely and tall her plants were. "Wow, everything is growing so much faster down here. You've done a great job on your garden! I'm from up north, and my plants aren't at all that tall, yet."

"Oh, thanks. I love to garden." She said.

"Me too!" I said, thinking I was sparking up a new friendship.

"Where are you from?" questioned the Yellow Springer.

"I don't know if you've ever heard of it." I paused before I continued with the words I've said about a zillion times in my life, "A little island in the Western Basin of Lake Erie called Put-in-Bay?" "Oh," she said with a slight giggle, "we call that place "Pick-up-Bay!" She followed with more giggles.

I went into defensive mode. It was as if she had just talked trash about my mother! And, to top it all off, she thought this was funny! With her comment, she quickly became my enemy.

I tried as best I could to respond in a well-mannered, sophisticated way, "Well, actually, I'm a 5th generation islander, and I have raised my kids there, teach school there, and the lake is really, really pretty."

Did she actually care that I was a 5th generation islander? Of course not! And, the way I described the island? I should have talked to her about our loving school. I should have filled her in on the history of the area. I should have shown her pictures of my two daughters. I should have laughed at her comment. I should have...I should have....

I don't even recall what she replied to my awkward attempt to define what Put-in-Bay is to me. Using the most polite voice I could summon, I said, "Goodbye! Happy Gardening!" and got the heck outta there. My mom had taught me to be polite. [After all, parents of "fill-in-the-blank-Bay" teach their children manners, for goodness sake!]

I continued my walk that day and felt much frustration due to the label that had been bestowed upon my island home.

What could I do in my lifetime that could possibly change the vision of what some think of Put-in-Bay? Does the average visitor know that our school not only boasts great test scores but also has some of the most dedicated teachers around? What about our amazing theatrical productions that the school kids organize, direct, and star in each winter? Do they know about Tip Niese's generosity each year at Christmastime?

Is there really anything I can do to change the thoughts of other people? No. But what I *can* do is share stories with all my readers. I can tell you about the vital lessons I've learned. I can share the best memories of my Island Girl life. Sometimes I do this with a bit of sarcasm in an attempt to bring humor to my writing. Through it, I can do my best to correct the impressions some people have of this amazing little place I call home.

I do love to write, and do so on scraps of paper daily and scribble in several journals (and I do mean *scribble*…have you ever tried to read my handwriting?). Post-it notes are my favorite place to put my thoughts—just ask my students. For me, writing has mostly been a very private part of me until now. I am so grateful that I get to share my thoughts in my column "Island Girl" in the Put-in-Bay *Gazette* with readers near and far.

Throughout my recent years of travel, I have also heard many other comments about Put-in-Bay. Perhaps you've heard them as well. The one that I took way too personally went something like this, "You wouldn't know about that—you've lived on an island your whole life."

Truth is, I do know a thing or two. I'll admit, there are many experiences that I didn't have growing up here: a prom, days at the mall, or a date at a drive-in movie (my first one was only two years ago). But the life I have led here has been, and still is, filled with other amazing experiences. And, these have helped me learn some very important lessons.

So, I've decided in this new year that I will try to keep it positive and very real. I will try not to complain about my island (too much) anymore. I will try to keep sarcasm to a minimum. Instead, during the year 2013, I am going to write about the things I've learned on this little rock. And I will share those lessons and other grateful memories, too. The Island of Put-in-Bay has been my classroom for almost 40 years, and I may, from time to time, complain about it—but don't you *dare*!

23

THE CHICKEN MAN

CONTINUED MY SOBBING AS I scooped seven little dead chickens out of the hen house with the shovel I normally use to transplant flowers. I had already put the information of The Chicken Massacre out on Facebook and even asked Aunt Betty (Parker) Bruening in Arizona if there were weasels on the island when she was a young island girl. Ty Burgess thought it was a raccoon, and my mom was already here, partially to console me and to check out the coop to look for openings that we may not have noticed. Nothing. Not a one. The only thing it could be was a weasel. Or a mink. Do we have such animals here? According to those at the Wildlife Center, the answer is, "No." It was a raccoon.

Are those darn raccoons actually *that* smart? Could they have gone inside that coop, then conveniently latched everything back up after leaving, so as to put the blame on those non-existent weasels and minks? Personally, I think it had to be a mink. Maybe it swam over like the deer? If you see me wearing a furry coat this winter, then you will know I was right.

As I continued to rake up their white and brown feathers, my mind actually did start to drift to a happier place. Back to the time when I first fell in love with those darned birds. [Why do I have to love them so much?] Many islanders actually had or still have poultry. In ye ol' days of our island times, it was for survival, and today it's more for the enjoyment and, of course, those great tasty eggs. Mary Ann McCann, Rick and Debbie Harlan, the Stacy family, and Marie Schroeder are some of the names that come to me. I think all the aforementioned families would agree that raising chickens brings enjoyment, sometimes frustration, and gratification when those eggs are eaten for breakfast. The Burgess family had chickens. I recall seeing the little baby chicks, and I distinctly remember this experience when I was a young girl. Holding them, hearing them peep. Ahh!…

My first learning experience with chickens was during my time living on Mitchell Road. Our neighbor Mr. Howard Scott had hens. He adored them as I do mine, and we always relished the fresh eggs. We would watch the late Mr. Scott go out to his coop each morning and even during the coldest days of winter, to take care of them. When I was a teenager, I used to think the old guy was nuts. Then, when I was his neighbor during my 20's with two young daughters, my opinion of him and his chickens quickly changed.

My oldest daughter, Anna, loved Mr. Scott and his flock of birds. She would follow him out to the coop, help him feed the hens, collect eggs, and scrape the floor of the coop to keep it extra clean. She would listen to him call his hens. Two of them were named Annie and Whitey (due to her pure white feathers). Mr. Scott spoke to those chickens every day.

"Here, Annie!" He would call as the day ended, "Get on your roost, chickens. Time for sleep, Whitey."

Then, five-year-old Anna would repeat, "Get on your roost, chickens!"

Meredith, my youngest, was a bit more hesitant. A big

chicken (pun intended), she would watch safely from a few feet away. She would only go into the coop if I were holding her. Anna's little friends would visit the chickens, too, because that was the thing to do when you were five years old. Young Dustin Franklyn, son of Tammie Campbell, visited one day and, after that, began calling Mr. Scott "The Chicken Man."

The Chicken Man had it all figured out. His coop was secured using lots of chicken wire, and at night, like clockwork, the hens would stroll back to the shed that he had turned into a chicken coop. They were safe from hawks due to the overhanging plants on the top of the outdoor cage. Inside at nighttime, they were locked in behind two solid doors. He was an expert.

Not only did he have knowledge of chickens, but he also enjoyed gardening, taking care of his wife, Alice, and knew how to live happily. Walking-stick in hand, he would meander down Mitchell Road, turning left onto Catawba into town and back home again. His walks were a necessity to him. His golf cart took him to Heineman's Winery often, and he always wore a big smile upon his return. I watched him out the window of our house as he trained my dog, Fair, at the side of his yard, teaching her to stay and wait for her treat. I hoped then, as I do now, that I can live as good and as long a life as the late Mr. Scott.

When his wife fell ill with cancer, he made sure she was comfortable inside their own home, and he kept a constant vigil over her. One time, when he had to go to the Island General Store, he wanted to be sure she was watched over, so I came to their house to sit beside her. I learned so much about true love then. Alice passed away about 16 years ago, but in time to see my oldest daughter take her first steps and count most of her baby teeth as they came in. Mrs. Scott loved children, as did her husband.

Mr. Scott was thoughtful and always remembered my

daughters' birthdays. He would get them the latest toys at Christmas time, and he knew what they wanted because he talked to them often. He spent a holiday or two in our kitchen with us. He made Anna and Meredith laugh, was patient with them, and taught them about nature.

Now, whenever I'm out at my chicken coop, and something terrible happens like The Chicken Massacre of 2012, I always think, WWMSD—What would Mr. Scott do? I already know the response because I can hear him telling me, "Christie, you have to seal those doors so they close tighter, and that wire is much too large." He would also feel my sadness at the loss of such dear pets.

Cliff never got the chance to know Mr. Scott, but he hears about him all—and I mean *all*—the time from me. I'm always referring to my previous neighbor when chicken farming. "Mr. Scott fed them this way," I say as I scatter their daily feed. "Mr. Scott's chickens would molt from time to time," I remind Cliff when I see some of our hens losing their feathers. And—too many times, "Mr. Scott did it *this* way."

I know what this island man taught me continues on. I think of him often and with love as I take care of our flock. When outside in my gardens, I think of how he tended lovingly to his. I try to remain happy and be thoughtful, as he was. I attempt daily exercise, and of course, love chickens. His daughter, Mindy, who resides in the same house as the famous Chicken Man on Mitchell Road, now gets to enjoy our fresh eggs. I hope she visits us when our new day-old hatchlings—that I ordered after a week of mourning—arrive at the post office!

24

MY SMART COMMUTE

I WANTED TO DRIVE MY new Smart car to work one September morning but remembered it was "Bike, Board, or Walk to School" week. So, I slipped on my dressiest pair of Birkenstocks and headed down Thompson Road. I was going to be a good role model for my students as they saw me walking that day. I do enjoy a walk or bike ride, but truthfully, this week, I was a little bummed. I just wanted to drive my new car with the "Got Aloha" decal on the back window.

I left the house early (I don't know how that happened…) and was able to calmly sip my freshly-ground French Vanilla coffee along the way. With each step, I began to think of how good I've got it. I get to live within a mile of my work, making my trip only about ten minutes when I walk, and I've been commuting to this school for nearly my whole life! As an adult, I take almost the same exact route I took as a young island girl.

As I meandered past Heineman's Winery, the familiar yummy smell of fall grapes wafted through the crisp morning air to my nose. "They must have been bottling all night," I said aloud as if someone were walking right beside me. Eddie and all his employees are some of the hardest working people on the island. I see them morning, noon, and night on my way to and from school.

I turned right onto Mr. Heineman's driveway. [I just love taking that little shortcut.] The mighty trees give me a sense of security, and the old building, where they used to take cave tours, still sits as if it wants to tell me stories of long ago. I gave that old building a smile, and I felt it grin right back at me.

As I walked along the old crumbling sidewalk in front of The Goat, I thought of it as my little challenge not to slip. The rain had fallen the night before, and so it was extra muddy, but I succeeded—no slipping! At the bottom of the hill, I practically skipped around the puddles that had accumulated the night before. My walk continued on past Cooper's Woods, and it was then that the memories came flooding back of my morning trips to school while growing up on the island.

Actually, I don't think my parents *ever* took us kids to school in a car. And, we didn't have golf carts or 4-wheelers then. An occasional ride on the back of my dad's snowmobile—*maybe*... but even then, there were three of us young Ontkos, and we all couldn't fit on the back of that thing. Yes, I was the kid who walked uphill *both* ways to and from school each day. I'm not even making this up. There *were* two hills on my trek to school. One was on Mitchell and the other on Catawba Rd.

I'm not trying to make my parents sound mean, just simply stating the facts. We got a ride to school when it was raining or very cold, but besides that, we Ontko kids were on our own. We only lived about half a mile from school, so of course we could walk or ride bikes. It would be silly to waste the gas.

I remember being so excited in first grade when I was heading off to my first official year of schooling. [No kindergarten then.] I was going to be like my big brother, Davey, who would ride his bike to school. At first, my mom gave me a test to see if I was ready. But I failed. She told me to ride up our street on Mitchell Rd., turn around, and come back down the hill. I did just that. I was so proud of myself! But when I got back to the front yard, my mom told me I wasn't ready. I was shocked and very upset.

"Why, Mom?" I said as I held back tears.

"Because you turned around up there at the top of the hill without looking behind you to see if a car was coming," she replied.

After the first failed bike-riding test, I got to have a redo about a week later. This time I remembered what my mother had taught me, and I passed with flying colors. Now, my young world opened up to new and exciting freedom!

As young kids, riding our bikes was the best way to get to school. And we just didn't ride our bikes via the roads; we often took a portion of Shady Path, making the trip fun and full of daring twists and turns on the rocky terrain. The four-minute bike ride turned into our morning adventure as we took a right into Cooper's driveway (now The Goat) and then into what was like a secret passageway into Shady Path.

Down the short hill from Cooper's, leading directly onto the wooded path we rode: my brother on his dirt bike, I on my three-speed blue Schwinn, and my little sister trailing somewhere behind. It wasn't long before we would meet up with my Luecke cousins, who had begun the Shady Path bike ride all the way from the beginning of the trail, on Thompson Rd. And, of course, our neighbors, the Riddle kids, were not too far behind us on their bikes. That made for about nine kids every morning riding over the dirt in Shady Path, enjoying their rides to school.

One morning, while riding my bike, I remember hitting a rock as I was cruising down the short wooded hill from the "secret" entrance to Shady Path. All my books fell right out of the basket, and at the same time, I flew off my Schwinn and crashed. Knowing I had to be at school, there was no time for crying. With the help of my cousin, Jimmy Luecke, I got back on my bike, and we got my books back inside my basket. I quickly swept the dirt off my jeans, and off we went.

That crash didn't stop me from loving Shady Path. It was great to walk in, too. As I entered my teen years, I would often take the trail. Sometimes, after school, I would take Shady Path the whole way to Thompson Rd. and then head home after that. I didn't even mind the extra few minutes it took me. Taking a walk through those woods just allowed me time to enjoy nature and be alone.

My parents were smart to make us ride or walk to school! Making us find our own way to school taught us responsibility. We could leave the house whenever we wanted, but we had to be on time for school. Our teachers were good at keeping track of those who were tardy. I didn't ever want to be "that late kid." The short walk or bike ride gave us a transition from home to school and was a great way to sneak exercise into our daily lives. Plus, taking Shady Path made for fun on the way to and from school.

So, thanks, Mom and Dad, for making me ride my bike or walk uphill both ways to school. Also, thanks to Amy Huston, who organized the "Bike, Board, or Walk to School" campaign. She reminded many children, parents, and me of the joy of a quiet and healthy commute to our island school. I will try to be smarter and leave my new little car in the driveway at home. But if you happen to see the little Smart car in the school parking lot, please know that there was a good reason for me to drive it to school that day.

25

CONNECTIONS

CLIFF AND I FLEW to Colorado recently to attend the high school graduation of my cousin, Greg Bruening's youngest child. Her name is Anneliese, and she is also my goddaughter. For nearly eighteen years, I've been sending small gifts and cards to her in the hopes of making a special connection, and of course, to fulfill my godmotherly duties. For all these years, I would get a thank you note written back to me each time. Her mom, Brenda, would often send me the latest school picture of my goddaughter, and they would go in a little frame on my desk, each one layered on top of the other.

A few years ago, I finally got to meet her for only the second time. The first was when my sister, Natalie, got married on the island, and at the time, Anneliese was a young girl, and I was so busy with the wedding, I didn't get much time with her. The second meeting was at our big Kuemmel Family reunion, only a few summers ago. We made an instant connection then— grown woman to teenage girl. Ever since, the small gifts and cards had become that much more personal.

As I boarded the plane in Cleveland, I had no idea what was in store for this short visit. I hardly know my goddaughter, but at the same time, I feel as if I've known her forever. My grandmother is her great-grandmother. All of the family history I have knowledge of, Anneliese barely knows. Since she has been raised in Boulder and has only visited Put-in-Bay twice in her whole life, we have lots of interesting topics that we can share throughout the weekend.

In Chicago, Cliff and I had to grab a connecting flight, and on this flight we couldn't sit next to each other. So there I was, seated between two young kids in their early twenties. Now that Cliff was nowhere near me, I had to chat with someone—right? The kid to the right of me didn't want to talk; I could tell from his body language as he had covered his ears and closed his eyes. The kid to the left of me sneezed, and in a motherly sort of way, I offered him a tissue.

"Thanks," he said.

"Allergies?" I inquired. "I know all about them. My youngest daughter has horrible allergies."

"Yup," he continued, "They have been really bad in Connecticut, where I go to school. But not so bad at home in California."

And then we were off! No stopping us now! This guy seated to the left of me was going to be my seat buddy for the next two and a half hours. I thought I'd better make the best of it.

"So, where in California are you from?" I asked.

"My parents actually just moved from a house in San Diego to another new, smaller one. So I'm from there, but won't be going home to the same house I grew up in. It's going to be kinda' weird."

"Yeah, I'll bet. But, at least you'll be in the same area—right?"

"It's okay," he explained. "I actually don't hang out with the people from my old neighborhood anymore anyway. Going off to college really changed me—in a good way."

He went on to explain the details of his mom and dad's new

house and how his dog would be waiting for him. I listened to him as if I were his young mom. (Yes, I said *young*…I'm only forty—remember?) This kid had just completed his third year in college and was going to be twenty-three soon. He had earned a scholarship to play basketball at his college in Connecticut, and appeared to be a good kid.

Finally, the question I'd been waiting for. The one that always comes.

"Where are you from?" he inquired.

I thought about it for a nanosecond. Should I really tell him I from the island of Put-in-Bay? Do I really want to go into this long explanation of what it is that I do, who I am, and what the island is all about? Or, should I just say, "I'm from the Cleveland area."

What the heck, he seems nice, and we've got two and a half hours.

"I'm from a small island in Lake Erie called Put-in-Bay."

"I've heard of Lake Erie," he says.

Thank *God*! I thought. At least I didn't have to tell him where the Great Lakes are located. And, then I went on to explain the importance of a great battle that took place right off our shores called "The Battle of Lake Erie." I also began telling him about our tall National Monument, when all of a sudden, the guy in the seat ahead of us turns his head around and says:

"Put-in-Bay? You're from that party island?"

This must be a test. I thought. Did somebody plant this guy near me? Did he know with whom he was dealing, here?

Nope. I wasn't gonna do it. I wasn't gonna' get defensive. Instead, I laughed a bit, gave him a gentle punch in the side of his bicep (or what was supposed to be a muscle), and asked, "Where are you from?"

"I'm from Chicago." He replied.

"Oh, what a great city," I offer before asking, "When were you on Put-in-Bay?"

"I've never been there, just heard of the place."

"Oh...so you've never even seen the island before?"

"Nope." The strange Chicago man said.

Perfect. I have been seated next to two people on this plane. I have the ability to teach them about our island and who I am. I can't let this one pass. I'm going in....

I quickly handed him one of my new business cards. The one that reads, "Freshwater Retreat—An Island Wellness Experience."

"Well, I hope you can make it there someday," I continue on. "Maybe you can stay with us at our new retreat? The island is a beautiful place. Our state park has amazing camping—I've actually camped there myself! You can plant your tent up on top of these gorgeous rocks and hear the sound of the lake all night long."

Chicago man snickers a little and smiles as he says, "I've been meaning to get there one of these days."

"*Great!*" I tell him. "I'd be happy to have you at my new place, and if you choose to indulge in some relaxing party time, that's fine—just be respectful of the house; it's over 150 years old! The island is a great place to come and release tension, get away from it all, or just relax." [I sounded like a commercial now....]

The college kid chimes in, "My girlfriend and I have been talking about staying at a bed and breakfast."

"Well, check me out on the web. Even if you don't come, at least I can see that someone in California has clicked on the site."

"Okay," he agrees.

Then, so that I don't have to do all the talking, I ask the college kid what he plans to do after school. "Basketball?" I inquire.

For the next two hours and fifteen minutes, I listen intently to him talk about his love for his girlfriend. He shows me pictures. He tells me about his dog, and I get more pictures. I show him the latest picture of my youngest daughter, Meredith, heading to prom, all pretty in her white dress. We have an enjoyable conversation, in which I play a little bit of Life Coach. The 6'6" kid and I both depart the plane feeling lighter and happy. And, the trip seemed to fly by....

As I depart, I say to Chicago Man, "Check out my website! I've got an amazing picture of the sunset on the island as my home page."

We landed in sunny Denver, and my goddaughter and Brenda were there to pick us up in the family minivan. A short car ride to Boulder and, ahh!...the mountains and scenery are just breathtaking. I feel an instant connection with Colorado.

After spending time with the Bruening family, seeing the quaint town of Boulder, and visiting Celestial Seasonings Tea Company, Cliff says to me, "Christie, you should've been born here. It so fits you!"

I can't believe I'm thinking it, but after forty years of trying to leave the island, get outta town, and make my way in the world, I keep getting these recurring messages. I am supposed to be here. Maybe so that I can promote the wonderfulness of our little island to people sitting next to me on planes; cousins in Boulder, Colorado; and all readers of the *Gazette*. Every time I leave Put-in-Bay, I feel so much pride to be from here. I am also so glad to get back after each and every trip. Besides, my chickens miss me whenever I travel. [I can just tell.]

26

AULD LANG SYNE

Should auld acquaintance be forgot
And never brought to mind?
Should auld acquaintance be forgot,
And auld lang syne!

M
Y PANDORA RADIO IS playing once again at this holiday time, and I hear James Taylor's melodic voice singing the lyrics above. I look forward to celebrating the New Year once again here on the island. Many seasonal songs will be played, and maybe I'll even hear that traditional song from the stage at Tipper's. I will listen to the lyrics and get a little weepy as I reminisce about friends who have come and gone on the island. My whole life, I've seen people come and go, and I still miss so many of them.

One of these memorable people is Claudette Moore, who was like a long-lost sister to me during her short stay on the island. She was a teacher's aide, while her husband, Ralph, was our Perry's Monument superintendent. This past Christmas, I thought of her as I decorated the Norfolk Island pine tree in my classroom. It was Claudette who had left it to me when she and Ralph set out for Alaska. I sent her a picture of it when it was fully decorated, as I knew she would approve. Claudette left such a positive impact on me during her short time on the island. We used to talk about holistic healing, education, children, as well as life in general, sharing much laughter along the way. I can still hear her eastern accent in my head as I think of her. Recently, she even ran the Boston Marathon! She continues to inspire me all these years later.

Coincidentally, another wonderful big-sister-like friend of mine, Tami Campbell, left that big Norfolk pine tree with Claudette before *she* moved off the island. Tami is now living happily with her husband, Al, making and selling her crafty creations all around the United States. So much talent! For years I worked for her as a babysitter to her son, Tavis, and then later, at Hortnords, the famous hot dog stand she owned, located on The Boardwalk. She taught me about independence and never judged my teenage actions/mistakes. Being my first boss, she also taught me the importance of treating employees like family and giving them love always. I strive to be that type of person in my business as well as at school, where I get to be the "boss" of my classroom.

Babysitting came naturally to me, as I've always loved children. The first person I ever babysat for was Melanie Duff. She has three children: Allison, Kevin, and Erin. I used to teach them how to clean their playroom when I babysat, and Melanie was always so appreciative. She paid me $5.00 an hour, which at the time was a huge amount! She always told me how much she trusted me and made me feel welcome in her home. Melanie often reminded me that babysitters were underpaid, and I remembered this when it was my turn to pay the girls who babysat for me, years later. She is now living just across the water in Port Clinton and, a while back, I ran into her at the Kroger, there. We caught up quickly and dove right into life's issues, such as marrying in mid-life and raising kids. It was great talking to her again!

When I was a child, one of my favorite moms was Mrs. (Cyndee) Altoff. She always had so much patience with me, and it was with her that I learned about worldly things—such as how to use chopsticks! Growing up in Hawaii (her mom still lives there), she and her hubby, Mr. Gerry Altoff, ended up on Put-in-Bay because he worked for the National Park Service at Perry's Monument. Her daughter, Kristin, and I quickly became besties after meeting when we were in elementary school. Years ago, on a visit to the island, Mrs. Altoff encouraged me to travel to London, England, to meet up with Kristin, where she was living at the time. What a trip that was, complete with a life-changing moment of clarity! Mrs. Altoff was and still is only 30 years old in my eyes. According to her Facebook posts from her home in Virginia, she is still doing well and enjoying life with Mr. Altoff.

Mrs. Robison, another parent whom I admired, did so many things in our community. She was a business owner and a teacher, as well as a single mom to two kids I grew up with: Zac and Jennifer. But it wasn't until my high school years that I really got to know Mrs. Robison. She was instrumental in getting many of us high school kids to attend weekend trips to mainland church conferences. On those weekends, we flourished as teens and got to express ourselves in ways we couldn't do otherwise. We all met mainland kids and in a safe environment, grew together, and got to talk about God and spirituality and stuff. [My favorite topics.] Later, Mrs. Robison got married to Mr. Mountain and, after a while, they left the island.

Whoever comes, let them come.
Whoever stays, let them stay.
Whoever goes, let them go.

I found this quote recently, changing it only slightly. I believe people enter our lives when we need them to and leave when it's time. It's that simple. But I still bawl my eyes out anytime an old friend moves far away. When Claudette Moore left the island, I wished her farewell through a river of tears in front of the house that she and Ralph shared near The Monument. She left over ten years ago, but the lessons I learned from our friendship together are still with me each day, and especially when I hear James Taylor's voice on the radio at holiday time.

To all of you with whom I've crossed paths in Put-in-Bay over the years, your positive imprint is still here. I will raise a glass to you this New Year's Eve. Cheers!

27

FIRST LOVE

I STILL HAVE THE SMALL tin box that was given to me when I was in fifth grade. I see it each morning as I get ready for my day because it sits on top of the medicine cabinet in my bathroom. On its round lid, there is an image of two little gnomes fixing a broken baby chick's leg. Hmm...maybe it was a premonition of what lay ahead in my adult life. I now have chickens and a gnome statue in my garden! Gnomes were one of my favorite things when I was a little girl, and my first island boyfriend knew this about me. You see, the little tin was a gift from him.

I hate knick-knacks—more to dust around. So, why do I still have that little knick-knack in a place that I see every day? The answer is that it reminds me of the simpler times of my young Island Girl life. It proves to me that even as a little girl with the big gap between my two front teeth and severely chewed up fingernails, someone cared about me. This small token of love is exactly the reminder I want to see when I begin my day!

My young admirer would write me love letters and give me small gifts at school. In fact, he gave me two gnome tins— the second one is a smaller rectangular one. When you slide it open, several small red confetti hearts are revealed.

This boy and I enjoyed each other's company. We laughed as we built forts together in the woods in September. When my friends and I picked him up for trick-or-treating, he was dressed up as Teddy Roosevelt. One snowy January, as he was sledding down the hill, he hollered, "Will you be my girlfrieeeeeend?" It was official. We were "going together" as we stomped around in our Moon Boots.

We never held hands or kissed—*gross*! Nobody did that in fifth grade! We didn't really *go* anywhere together. Most of the time, we were in a group with other friends as we "went together."

He was kind and smart. His freckles, red hair, and plaid shirt stand out in his sixth grade school picture that I still have inside a trunk in the attic, along with his love letters. He was just a kid like me, wanting to feel that strong emotion of first love.

When he moved off the island, I remember being so very sad. I told my friend, Libby, about my sorrow one afternoon, as we were walking on the way to Girl Scouts. I'm not even sure where he moved to. I just remember at the time, he was living with his grandparents and was told he had to relocate to the mainland to be with his dad.

This boy is now a man, all grown up with a family of his own, and looks very happy in all the Facebook pictures I see. I'm pretty sure he doesn't read the *Gazette*, but I'm guessing some of his relatives who still live on the island might just read this. Who knows?

I do know that I'm still holding onto love. Love for that little girl with the gap between her teeth and for boys who still give their first girlfriends love letters, though today they send love "texts." I get to witness first love appearing every day in my classroom full of fourth, fifth, and sixth graders. Some things never change.

Most of all, today I am grateful for the gift of winter days filled with love and Valentines. The excitement of this day, as seen through the innocent eyes of my students as they hand me their homemade works of art is a memory I will cherish forever.

Happy Valentine's Day!

28

GRAMMA'S SALVE

WHEN I WAS A young girl, I earned many a scraped knee. Whenever I would injure myself, there was no fancy Neosporin in the medicine cabinet. Instead, we had Gramma's Salve, a medicinal ointment made first by my great grandmother, Christina Parker. It was a yellowish type of gunk in a small plastic medicine bottle. On the bottle was a label made from masking tape that read "Chris's Salve—a lot to draw, a little to heal." I really didn't know what "draw" meant, except for what I attempted in art class. I did know, however, that I wanted my boo-boo to feel better. So, I'd stick my finger inside that bottle, get some goop, and put it on my injury. In moments I'd be back out the door again, playing with our neighbors, the Riddle kids.

This stuff had an amazing smell—so unique that I couldn't describe it. It didn't smell like anything pretty, but I loved it! Not like flowers or anything like that, but the odor always made me feel better upon opening the bottle. With its distinct smell, I knew the healing would begin once applied.

I was eager to find out more about my great grandmother, creator of the salve. Who was this woman who had secret healing recipes? After two years of begging my mom for the family recipe and finally getting it, I ordered the ingredients to make this healing salve (thank God for the Internet!). At the family dinner that evening, I brought the conversation to the long-ago times of the Parker family of Put-in-Bay.

"Mom, do you remember your grandmother?" I asked.

"No, I only remember her funeral. I remember Aunt Annie's big hat that she was wearing that day," Mom said, smiling at Aunt Annie, who was also at the table that night.

Aunt Annie didn't comment about the hat but began telling me all about our Parker family. I'd heard the stories about how they arrived here from England but didn't know about my ancestor's personalities or how they lived their lives here on the island. Aunt Annie knew my grandmother well. She was married to Christina Parker's youngest son, Joe Parker (in case you can't see the family tree in your mind, that would make my great-grandma my Aunt Annie's mother-in-law).

I knew my great grandmother bore 12 children. Her face was clear to me from an old black-and-white family photo that hangs on my mom's wall. She looked so tired in that picture. I also knew that her maiden name was German. Something inside me was eager to learn as much as I could about my great-grandmother, mother to my grandfather, Alfred. This woman had inspired me to order ingredients from the Internet that I'd never even heard of before and to become a chemist one weekend in my kitchen!

So, great aunt Annie Parker was my go-to lady because she knew so much. She not only had known Christina Parker but had actually performed a skit in which she portrayed her! The following is a slightly modified version of the script my Aunt Annie Parker wrote. I think it does a wonderful job of describing the woman my great-grandmother was and could well have been what she might have written herself.

Good day. I am Mrs. Christina Parker. My husband, Jobe, was a grape farmer. We never made much money at that.

But the children worked and we were able to manage. Some winters, there was not one dollar to rub against the other. I often felt I couldn't afford a one-cent stamp to write to my parents in Sandusky. We charged our groceries at the general store all winter and paid for them the following summer.

We canned many quarts of fruits and jam and jelly. We stored our garden vegetables and apples and sauerkraut in the root cellar. We had a cow and chickens. Each year we raised a hog to butcher in the fall. Joey, my youngest son, still says nothing ever tasted better than that fresh sausage. The boys hunted in the fall and we all loved eating those rabbits and pheasants. We ate plenty of fish in those days.

Every Saturday I baked a week's supply of bread and kuchen (coffee cake) and fried doughnuts. Little Joey loved store bread and all his life did not care for homemade. I often cooked knepfles (spaetzle).

I earned extra money by taking in washing and ironing, doing sheets and tablecloths for the hotels, including the Hotel Victory. I was pregnant with Joey when that hotel burned down in 1919.

I was an excellent seamstress and after the other work was done, often sewed at night by kerosene light. I could take apart an old garment and turn it inside out to cut a smaller coat or jacket from it.

One time I did a beautiful mending job on Joey's trousers. He refused to wear them to school so I pointed out that Howard Ingold wore patched pants and his parents were well off. Joey said, "I don't care if he does—I don't." And he didn't.

When we moved to town from the farmhouse, it was wonderful to have electricity, running water, an indoor bathroom and a real washing machine. Before that we used a washboard.

I first came to the islands from Sandusky to pick grapes at Middle Bass when I was 18. There I met Jobe Parker who was 27. He asked me to correspond with him. I said "All right, if you write to me first." We were married the following year.

Of our five sons and seven daughters, four were born in October—grape harvest time. I was in the vineyard picking grapes on those days. I later went into the house and the midwife was summoned.

Our oldest son was Harold. Our youngest daughter, Rita, was four. Twelve total Parker children were raised on the island of Put-in-Bay.

Another son Earl, was also known as Skinny. He worked for Kinsler's Blacksmith Shop and gas station as a mechanic. He later started his own station in the little building by our home, which was once Local Color. (The house that sits directly behind Cameo Pizza.) After WWII he built Parker's Garage where the building that houses Isola Day Spa and other places are today.

Long before that, my husband's sister, Fannie Rittman, ran the Hotel Perry located on the corner across from Tony's Garage.

One of my other sons was named Alfred. You may have known him as Captain Parker of the Erie Isle, Yankee

Clipper, and Parker Boat Line. Before that, he, too, was a grape farmer, and was foreman of the E & K Vineyards on the island. He and his family lived where the Barnhills now have their Vineyard Bed and Breakfast.

I had a daughter named Christine. When she was 15 years old, she had to drop out of school and moved to the Gascoyne home where the Kelly Faris Family now lives. This was a farm and as the hired girl, she had to do all the washing and cooking and cleaning for the family and their many farm hands. She came home on weekends and gave me all but 50 cents of her pay. I don't know what she did with all that money. She later married Jim Rudy and for many years they were caretakers at Frohman Lodge, now the Graves' home.

Joey's first job at age 11 was selling ice and bait at Miller Boat Livery six and a half days a week in summer. He had Sunday mornings off to go to Mass.

Only our three youngest children were able to graduate from Put-in-Bay High School because the older ones had to go to work full time after the eighth or tenth grade. It stopped them from being members of the Put-in-Bay High School Alumni Association, but it didn't stop some of them from becoming millionaires.

My husband, Jobe, died of skin cancer. We never knew if it was caused by the sprays he used on the grapes, or if it started when he once froze his face while crossing the ice from Sandusky. He had lost his cap and was riding on the running board in case the ice should break. Those were the days when we did that sort of thing much more often than today.

My husband died when I was in my early fifties. I still

had six children at home. And there was no widow's pension or Social Security in those days. Besides, Parkers were too proud to accept welfare!

When I was 62, my youngest daughter was 18, so my work of raising a family was accomplished and I could look forward to living alone in my little house, having a time of rest. But that year I suffered a stroke and from then on I walked with a cane and could not use my left hand. I couldn't live alone and was dependent on my children to help me with the simplest tasks such as dressing and combing my hair.

But I was still able to play pinochle using a special board my son Robert made for me. I was able to write with my good right hand and enjoyed corresponding with my children who had moved away from the island.

My Catholic faith meant a great deal to me. I knew that my suffering and hard work would help earn a place for me in heaven.

I often declared I would be happy to be "six feet under."

But I loved to work and cook and clean and we had many happy times. On Sunday afternoons, the children and their friends would gather and my husband would pop corn by the lard can full and everyone would laugh and talk and just have fun. There were card parties and bingo at the Town Hall.

I lived for 13 years after my illness. I was age 75 when another stroke took my life. Would I change my life as a grape farmer's wife for any other? I don't think so. I had a wonderful life, a wonderful family. And I thank God for all.

I never thought I would cry upon reading my Great Aunt Annie's story about my great-grandmother's life on Put-in-Bay, nor did I ever think I would feel so honored to be her great-granddaughter.

Maybe Gramma Christina was leaving something more than "a lot to draw, a little to heal" behind. Maybe she was leaving a legacy of healing, memories of her island life, and inspiration in me. I ended up making several renditions of the healing stuff. The first batch was the true Gramma's Salve. Then, I got creative and added some lavender from my garden. I tested out a few other renditions of healing salves and made those, too. On each jar, in honor of my grandmother, I labeled them "Gramma Christina's Salve" with a short description of what's inside each. With pride and love, I gave my first jar to my mom and the second to my Aunt Annie.

On this Mother's Day, I implore you to ask about your mother and the many mothers who came before her.

29

ISLAND PRINCESS

CLIFF AND I WERE out to dinner at the Crew's Nest, Put-in-Bay's boat club and resort, sitting under a nice umbrella enjoying our summer evening. That night, looking out over Lake Erie, I was in full gratitude for my Island Girl life. I love summer: hot days, cool nights, and more time to be with my loving companion, Cliff. The night prior to our Crew's Nest date, we had attended a cookout with my mom, her "Midnight Lady" friends, and all of our families. It's been another summer filled with friends and family.

Out of nowhere, this partner of mine decides to fill me in on his philosophy of what he and Kenny Harwood (Put-in-Bay '66) have coined, "Island Princess."

HIM: Christie, you're such an Island Princess.

ME: I'm not a princess. You must be mistaking me for my friend, Mainland Jen. She is the Princess. Remember her *gorgeous* wedding a few years ago at the Catawba Island Club? She is Princess Kate, and I'm Pippa, remember?

HIM: You're not getting it. You never go fishing with me, and you're deathly afraid of water snakes—and snakes in general.

ME: So…who *likes* water snakes? And when I'm gardening, and those snakes slither around—they freak me out!

HIM: Remember that wood spider in our bedroom the other night and how you screamed at the top of your lungs?

ME: *Hellllooooo!*—the spider was in our **bedroom**!

HIM: You're from an *island*—you shouldn't be afraid of any of them. You've been around snakes and spiders your whole life. And I'll bet you can't even bait a hook when out fishing, can you?

ME: No. And remember—I don't go fishing.

HIM: I think your dad has just spoiled you.

I thought about his comment for a second. Maybe my dad, Captain Charlie Tuna, *did* spoil me a little. I do recall feeling like royalty as I sat upon that tall, twirly chair, steering those big ferry boats. I got to march right up to the pilothouse when all the tourists had to sit in the regular seats. And, come to think of it, my Grandpa, Captain Alfred Parker, also used to allow me to do this, too. Hmm…I never had to pay, either. I probably sounded a little snobby as a young kid when telling everyone I didn't have to pay to ride the Parker or Miller boats. However, didn't every kid get to steer the boat? Now, onto this business about fish and other icky stuff….

ME: Well, I was too busy working in the summers to worry about baiting a hook. There wasn't time for such leisurely activities. And, in the winter—*yes*—my dad was with me in the ice shanty, so of *course* he would bait the hook for me.

HIM: (sipping his Crew's Nest cocktail.) He spoiled you.

There must be others like myself. My mind turns to my childhood friends, Libby and Emily Morrow. We were just together at our Midnight Ladies Family Reunion, and I remember us all out on the state park dock after dinner with about a million kids. Not one of us could remove the fish that one of the kids caught from the pole's hook. Too gross for any of us Island Girls. Cliff had to do it. And we were all pretty squeamish with those water snakes around in the water, my mom and Sue Latham included.

> **ME:** (getting a bit annoyed and defensive with my love) I can mow the lawn!

It's not my fault Cliff *likes* to do it! I used to mow my own lawn for years before he came along. In fact, I am amazing with the weed whacker. But should I fight a man who wants to take on this chore? Heck no! Why would anyone in her right mind want to argue over such a thing? I simply *allow* Cliff to mow the lawn now. I feel as if by doing this, he gets his manly shot of testosterone each time he is out there in the heat, pushing that thing around through the tall grass. Why would a nice Island Girl like me ever want to take that away from him?

He doesn't even want to debate this one with me. I think he hears me as I state the fact that I can mow the lawn, but he seems to be ignoring me. So, I continue with my defense.

> **ME:** I can use a power screwdriver and did so just the other day when I replaced two doorknobs at the retreat! [I didn't tell him that it took me over an hour to figure out why one wouldn't fit correctly.] I also helped my cousin Scott Parker when he remodeled the meditation room.
>
> **HIM:** You and I both know your cousin Scott did all the work, Christie.

He had a good point there. I was very good at zooming to the Island Hardware store in my Smart car to buy supplies for Scott. I was also very good at directing him on how I wanted the meditation room to look.

> **ME:** I can also drive a 4-wheeler with a shifter! In high school, P.J. Riddle had one, and he would let me ride it sometimes.
>
> **HIM:** A shifter? That's what you call it?

I'm really not getting what he means. And he paid no attention to my comment on the power tool usage and the doorknobs that I replaced—all by myself.

> **ME:** Yes, a shifter thing. It had a clutch on the footrest.

Ha, now I've got him convinced that I'm not an Island Princess! I used the word "clutch!" I am a smart woman, and I like to get creative with my vocabulary.

> **HIM:** Well, it's just like Kenny Harwood said at the Alumni Banquet: you came from an Island Princess—your mom. You just can't help being one.

Now he's got me stumped. Whatever does he mean?

> **HIM:** Remember how Kenny pointed out the fact that none of the island girls would date him or his brother Jim because they lived here? Kenny said the Island boys weren't good enough for your mom and her friends. They all had to date the Coast Guard boys, instead.

Ahh!...yes. Stories of Coast Guard boys have filled my mom's kitchen from time to time. Her eyes will glaze over as she talks about the days when the Coast Guard ships docked here. Even my Aunt Jeanette married a "Coastie." Uncle Tim Luecke was one of those handsome Coast Guard men.

I don't recall any Coast Guard cuties in my day, but I do

distinctly remember my first summer crush—a sailor boy by the name of Jeff. He was here during Junior Regatta on a boat called the *Banana Boat*. [I think it was because the boat was yellow—*very* original….] Even though I have never been sailing, just the thought of him out there on the lake was so romantic. The summer sun making his blonde hair that much lighter… oh, the memories! He wrote me about three letters that winter. I think he found a mainland girl after that. Silly him.

As for the island boys, I now recall my own teen years in which I didn't date anyone from high school. For heaven's sake, they were all like brothers to me!

I tried to date one boy. The kiss was just disgusting. I think it probably grossed him out, too. One kiss. That's how long we "dated." Does this fact make me an "Island Princess" or just a picky high school girl who had only three boys in my class to choose from?

> **ME:** Honey, let's just forget about all this Island Princess nonsense and enjoy the lake view tonight— shall we?

Then I ordered my meal: that delicious Crew's Nest broiled wedge salad. Yum.

But he couldn't let it go. For days after that, my every move was being analyzed to see whether or not it was "Princess-like."

As Cliff and I rode bikes to The Goat for lunch, there he was, swerving all over the road as if he owned it. He never follows the bike rules! You're supposed to stay to the right. You're supposed to use hand signals. And when a car comes, you're supposed to ride single file, so they can easily get around you. Doesn't everyone do this? Nope. Not Cliff. As he is being Mr. Hotshot on his bike, he begins again with this princess stuff after I give him a look that seemed to say, "You really should be following the bike rules!"

HIM: You even ride a bike like a princess! Your daughter, Meredith, does it as well. You both sit up straight, never removing your hands from both handles—ever. You both follow the traffic laws, too.

Why does this make us princesses? I think it makes us safe bike riders. And, yes, we sit up straight. Good posture. Okay, fine. Maybe we both ride bikes with princess-like behavior. I wonder if real princesses even ride bikes. Probably not. They get carriage rides everywhere.

During our lunch, I catch myself asking the waitress for two helpings of dressing for my Greek salad. I also ask for it on the side so that I can mix it with extra gyro sauce, which I've also requested. I'm beginning to think I sound like Meg Ryan from that 80's movie *When Harry Met Sally*. I did ask politely, though. And, I tip generously, having been a waitress once or twice in my life.

I love the fact that Caroline Koehler is there at The Goat, and she gives me a big smile and a wave every time I dine there. I always wave back and enjoy the fact that someone knows who I am almost everywhere I eat on this island. It's a good feeling. I sometimes get special treatment because I live here and just happen to know bartenders, waitresses, and business owners. Is that a bad thing? I think not.

As I receive the extra dressing for my salad, my mind returns to the first conversation Cliff and I had regarding my so-called royal blood. I can think of three amazing women who live here who are not princesses!

Theresa Finney is the first one who comes to mind. She loves to go ice fishing and probably even cleans the walleye she and her hubby catch. She posts pictures of those big, slimy things on Facebook all the time. And Kristin, the snake lady, *loves* those snakes! She has even been on TV promoting the love of those creatures with teeth. I'm pretty sure that Lisa Brohl loves the snakes, too!

But as Cliff quickly points out to me, they don't count because they weren't *raised* here. Darn. Foiled again. Who makes the princess rules, anyway? Obviously, Kenny and Cliff. Did Cliff remember that I have one of those "Save the Snakes" metal signs? Probably not. I forgot to point this fact out to him.

A few days after our lunch at The Goat, there was no more talk of royalty. I was grateful because I was getting tired of defending my actions. One of the toilets at my new retreat place was running, and I said something like this to Cliff, "Hey honey, there is a toilet that's running, and I'm paying for city water."

Thinking that he will eagerly jump up to fix it, he surprised me with the comment, "Well, take the lid off and have a look. Toilets are pretty easy to fix."

I was shocked. But, not wanting to exhibit any princess-like behavior, I didn't flinch and instead got up quickly to check out the running toilet. I took the lid off and played with some levers and other things inside the tank. I discovered that if you hold the handle down 'til all the way flushed, then it wouldn't run—as often. I carefully wrote a sticky note, "Hold handle until completely flushed" (like the ones you see in gas stations), so that all my retreat guests would know the trick of the running toilet. This whole process took about ten minutes. I was so proud of myself.

Flash forward to just the other day. The toilet was still running, and Cliff now decides to take notice. "Hey Christie!" he calls to me from the bathroom. "I turned off the water to that toilet tank until I can get time tomorrow to fix it. It's running pretty badly. [Oh *really*, I hadn't noticed.] I thank him lovingly anyway, "Thanks so much, honey!" I holler back.

Cliff fixed it the next morning. Crisis solved.

So, I've thought about this label. What's so bad about it? If this means I don't have to mow the lawn, get what I want when I'm out to eat, and have my toilets fixed, then—so be it. What's wrong with knowing most everyone when out to eat? What's wrong with following traffic rules? Lastly, I may someday get over my fear of snakes and huge spiders in my bedroom, but for now, I will keep them at a distance.

This whole story sorta reminds me of my first article in the *Gazette* called "A Horrible Islander." I guess all this time, I really haven't been a horrible islander, but instead, an Island Princess. There is a saying on my wall that I've passed about a thousand times. It reads, "It's not easy being a Princess, but hey, if the shoe fits...." I get it, folks—I'm an Island Princess. And, if you're an Island Girl, you may just want to climb aboard my royal carriage and become one, too.

30

LITTLE HOUSE ON THE LAKE

I AM ONE OF *THOSE* people. You know, the ones who play Christmas music the day after Halloween? Just ask my island students in fourth, fifth, and sixth grades. I love the holiday time, so I want it to last as long as possible—the longer, the better. During this time of year, the island lights up with festive parties, people are nicer (even to people they have had disagreements with), and it seems that everyone is just happier with life.

Each year I ceremoniously bring out a special VCR tape (yes, I said *VCR*). This movie is entitled *Little House on the Prairie: The Christmas They Never Forgot*. I highly recommend viewing this if you haven't recently. In the film, all of the show's main characters, now all grown up, get stuck inside on Christmas morning after a snowstorm. Since they can't go anywhere, they pass the time by sharing stories of their favorite Christmases on the frontier.

Every year when I watch it with my students, I think of our own little island of people and how much we are like the characters in this once-famous TV show.

Ma and Pa Ingalls were such loving people with patience, loved their children, and had a strong work ethic. In our island community, I feel that Paula and John Ladd fit the bill for this one. They are always so full of love each time I see them. Can't ya just visualize them at night with Paula in her nightcap discussing problems of the day with John? I can. Gotta love those people. Mrs. Ladd was a teacher at one time, as was Ma Ingalls. Mr. Ladd is oftentimes seen working in his yard, something I know Pa Ingalls did while tending his field.

In *Little House*, Mr. Edwards was the guy who saved the day, always helped a neighbor, and was so loved by the children of the Ingalls family. Don't you think our Richard Gump fits this description? Sometimes that Mr. Gump guy will help people, and nobody even knows it was he! Like the character, Mr. Edwards, who taught young Laura to spit out on the prairie, Richard taught me how to ride a motorcycle. Pretty similar, I'd say.

We have our very own Doc Baker, too. Actually, we are privileged to have *two* of them: Keith and Tami, at the EMS office. In fact, fifteen years ago, when my daughter was born, the pediatrician insisted that I weigh her each day. Keith and Tami kindly opened up their EMS doors to me each morning and helped me weigh my new little baby. And, like Doc Baker, they will come to your house, too. [Of course, we don't want that to happen because that would mean there was an emergency.] They are our island "docs," and we're lucky to have them!

The teacher on the show, Eliza Jane Wilder, is much like our own Amy Huston of Put-in-Bay School. She is always firm but full of love. Amy cares about her students and does her best to teach each child according to their individual abilities. A minor difference between the two characters is that Eliza did not have a dashing Peter Huston by her side, as Amy does.

Mother Mary is our very own version of Reverend Robert Alden. They are both cut from the same cloth—the Christian cloth, that is. Both wear smiles and help promote peace and love. They lead the community in goodwill and prayers. There was a friend of Pa's on *Little House* named Jonathan Garvey, who once had to explain to his wife why he had sold their horses. His answer was much like something Scott Pugh would say: "Providing for the needs of my family. What else is ever on my mind?" I think Scott would sell his company truck if he had to.

Then, there's Jonathan's wife, Alice, who was quoted as saying, "Oh, Jonathan, I love you so much. Thanks for putting the family first. You're an amazing husband." Now, I don't know if I would ever hear Kim Pugh say this—because as we all know, Scott does most of the talking—but I do believe Kim thinks that way often. Kim truly loves her husband, Scott.

The Olesons on *Little House* owned the town's grocery store. Even though Frieda is no longer with us here on Put-in-Bay, I think we'd all agree that she could take the place of both of the characters. She was always helpful, knew all the goings-on, and was very kind, just as Mr. Oleson was. Frieda was always on top of things at their grocery store, and I have no doubt that Maria will do an outstanding job, too!

Almanzo Wilder was the love of main character, Laura. [*Of course* this guy is Cliff.] Almanzo rescued the town from perishing one winter and saved the day numerous times on the television show. And he was so handsome! Like Almanzo, who gave Laura romantic rides home in a horse and carriage, Cliff has given me rides home in his pick-up truck.

Speaking of Laura Ingalls Wilder, I have to be her, folks. After all, she is the main character, and, as a child, I did have big teeth (with a gap, not an overbite) and brown hair, much like Melissa Gilbert, who played Laura on the show. So, I'll claim that character. She was also the middle child, as I am. She also became a teacher, loved writing, and went on to write and be published in her adult life. OMG—me too! So, I definitely get to be her.

Both the *Little House* books and the TV series stressed the importance of small-town people helping each other and getting through tough challenges—together. I truly believe that's why we are here on this tiny island called Put-in-Bay—to help and teach one another life lessons. I could name a hundred island events that have taught me how to be a better person, and I'm sure others on the island could, as well. We must be here for each other in good times and in bad because we're all we've got, folks!

Much like Mrs. Wilder, I've already written several chapters of stories from my childhood. They're inside a special basket in my bedroom, waiting for the book, TV, or movie deal to arrive. These stories speak much about my life on an island and are similar in feeling to those of *Little House* books. Maybe I should call my future book "Little House on the Lake." Nah, too corny. In the meantime, a sincere and most joyous Happy Holidays to all of my island friends, family, and neighbors. You may borrow my old VHS tape of *Little House on the Prairie*—just make sure you still own a VCR on which to view it.

31

CHRISTMAS *TIME*

THERE WAS A TABLE filled with brightly colored Christmas decorations while homemade desserts and cookies filled another. Jessie's handmade jewelry was displayed at the head table, and island girls, Kelly Dress and newlywed Michala sat on the opposite side, displaying their Stone Lab clothing. Caroline Jackson sold little succulent plants (adorbs) and island harvested lavender in sachets. It seemed as if the entire community came out to support our local artisans and non-profits. Amy Huston and Susan Byrnes organized another fabulous Christmas Bazaar sponsored by Lake Erie Islands Conservancy and the Lake Erie Islands Nature and Wildlife Center. Amy even sold out of her soup!

The Christmas Bazaar has been a tradition ever since I can remember. Mrs. Linda Mahony (the former Mrs. Goaziou, a teacher at Put-in-Bay School) was in charge, and I remember being so excited each year getting ready for this event! My excitement hasn't changed. When the Christmas Bazaar opens, it marks the beginning of the holiday season here on Put-in-Bay, and this writer couldn't be happier. *I love the Christmas holidays!* Especially when I'm here at home, on "my" little Lake Erie island, because it's the beginning of the winter months when things slow down and we all have more time. Christmas brings back memories of family togetherness. My dad would have time off from his ferryboat captain job, and my mom would be all done with the family business, too. No more 56-hour (or more) workweeks. It was so wonderful having both my parents at home during our lunch hour from school, and family dinners would become a regular occurrence once again. My dad would applaud and say at our meals, "Mom's a good cook!" and my big brother, Davey, and little sister, Natalie, and I would chime in, too.

There was more time for family, baking, and warm fires, and it's still that way today. Now, holiday time is when college daughter Meredith comes home for some R&R. I get to be with her each day and drive her nuts in the morning with all my loud noises making breakfast. Rattling all the pots and pans in the morning is my "thing." Not a moment to waste! The island holiday time is a time for me to take a stroll down memory lane with an impromptu stop at my mom's (I just have to be careful not to catch her at nap time.) Or, time to drive my little Smart car out to grown daughter Anna's apartment on East Point. She, too, gets to finally rest a bit from her long days managing Joe's Bar. And, I get to stop in unexpectedly. We all have more time.

Christmas is a time of community and cheer. Potlucks pop up, the school holds its Christmas concert, and house parties are the thing. Lights go up all around the island, and there's even a bit of friendly competition involving all the colorful decor. Fruit baskets are delivered to people aged sixty and over [OMG…in five short years, Cliff will be receiving one!] and often, there are carolers who travel around the island spreading their musical cheer. Santa arrives and gives a special gift to each island child. It's good to give, people. Do it! An island Christmas is filled with sharing.

Life is so hectic during the tourist season, and even though fall slows down a bit, we're still busy. Christmas marks the beginning of more time for us to really feel grateful for each other and feel a part of our island community. It's the time when the island comes alive with holiday cheer, sharing, and being together. We celebrate all the hard work from the summer months and give time to one another. If you're lucky, like me, you'll get to experience an island Christmas someday in your life.

32

WINTER BREAK

URING THE COLD WINTER months in the middle of February, each year, the island becomes an even more desolate place as a mass exodus occurs. I'm speaking of the time of year when our school takes its yearly winter break, during which many families take trips to southern shores or ski-sloped mountains. Some families use this time to catch up on their mainland appointments, while others choose to stay put (no pun intended) and enjoy the extra peace and quiet of the island. The winter break at our school can be a wonderful time for many island families!

In my sixteen years of teaching, I've heard stories every year about lucky students getting to travel on large cruise ships to places never seen by their teacher. I've heard of so many road trips to Florida that I've lost count. These students often come back to school after the break with sand still between their toes and peeling noses from a bad sunburn. One thing is for sure: they always come back a little refreshed—as does their teacher.

My own family has been blessed by this school vacation each February. My daughters have traveled with their dad each year, and they've had the privilege of boarding numerous cruise ships. Meredith learned how to barter for goods in places like

Mexico, and Anna always came back with an amazing tan...
along with a story of a boy she'd just met.

I, too, have been very blessed by this break. Just this past
February, our friends, Gordon and Kyle—who are now newly-
weds—let us use their condo in Siesta Key, Florida. I've traveled
across both oceans and had my dream experience last year in
Maui, Hawaii!

These adventures are a far cry from what my family did
when I was growing up here on the island. At that time, our
school didn't even have a winter break. Instead, my family chose
one weekend each winter when we would leave the island. Many
times, it was our one and only trip off-island during the winter.
Sometimes we would go with the Burgess or Morrow families.
It was awesome because my best friends were T.J. Burgess and
Libby Morrow!

Our destination: a hotel with an indoor pool. In Ohio.

First, we would board the old Ford Tri-motor. Due to
its smaller wheels in the back and three large motors in the
front, the plane was at such a slant when parked that I had to
walk uphill to get to my seat. I would climb past the rows of
seats and plant myself near the front so I could watch my big
brother. Davey usually got the co-pilot's seat, which was fine
by me. Those knobs and gauges everywhere scared me. What
if I bumped a button by mistake while in mid-air? What if I
accidentally turned the airplane off? [Was that even possible?]

As we flew off the island, we got to see the ice and shanties
below us, sometimes not flying much above it all. [I don't think
the FAA was as strict back then as they are today.] Those days,
there were no reservations for a flight. You simply went out
to the airport, hoping to hop on a plane. The key was getting
there early before all the ice fishermen arrived. Otherwise, you
might just be waiting all day. When we did get on, we were very

psyched to be leaving for our Big Winter Trip. Upon arrival, off we went on our mainland vacation!

First stop—McDonald's. This was our idea of fine dining in the Ontko Family. We rarely ever ate fast food because there weren't any such restaurants on the island. McDonald's was a big deal. I can still recall the day when I was able to eat a Big Mac all by myself. I was so proud! Now, I truly wonder what it was that I was so proud of. Most often, though, I ordered a double cheeseburger with extra pickles and fries. Root beer was my drink of choice. Pure sugar—and pure yummy!

Sometimes we would go to Sandusky, but if we were really lucky, Toledo, Ohio, was where we would end up. Maybe even a trip to the big mall! As a young child, I was a bit overwhelmed by all the people in a mall. It was so loud, as all the voices echoed back and forth under the high ceilings. But I still reveled in the fact that you could buy almost anything you wanted in that huge shopping place.

Maybe we would even see a movie! I remember getting to see *E.T.* in the theater. Cliff often asks me if I've seen a particular movie. My response to him is usually, "I grew up on an island. I didn't see many films." Now, with the help of Netflix, I'm slowly catching up on the movies that all the mainland kids grew up watching in theaters.

After eating fast food, shopping, and movie-going, my parents would sometimes splurge for the amazing hotel in Perrysburg, where the heated indoor pool met the outdoors. We could swim underneath the heavy plastic barrier, which hung down from a small area no larger than five feet across. Then we would be outside—in the middle of winter!

It was always a thrill to watch my big brother, Davey, get out of the pool and lie down in the cold snow. He would wow us all by making a snow angel, flapping his "wings" a few times before screaming and jumping back into the water. Other times, he would get out of the pool, only to cause trouble by throwing snowballs.

"Betcha can't get me!" I would tease as I slipped underneath the water. If he did manage to hit me, I would promptly run to find my mom or dad—and tell on him, of course.

"Mom, Davey is throwing snowballs into the pool at us!" I whined.

From the hot tub (she on was vacation, too!) came my mom's voice, "David, stop it!"

"Why are you such a narc?" My brother would ask me.

This would go on throughout the entire weekend. My brother caused trouble, and I—the goodie-goodie-tattle-telling sister—would tell on him. Our little sister, Natalie, just watched the interaction, not ever getting too involved (she was the smart one). Along with all the tattling and annoying sibling behavior, we would carefully plot out the best hallways in which to play hide-n-seek. We also would play a round or two of putt-putt.

But even if my parents had taken us on a big trip somewhere farther away, wouldn't we have experienced similar things? Don't siblings tell on each other on beaches in Florida? Kids argue with one another whether they are in this country or on a cruise ship. Sometimes, putt-putting is even on the agenda on a vacation. And normally, a trip to a warmer climate *does* involve swimming in water somewhere.

A trip to the mainland in wintertime was a big deal, not to mention a financial splurge for our family of five. What else does a kid need but a hotel with an indoor pool, golf course, and numerous hallways in which to play hide-n-seek? All I know is that I'm grateful to my parents for all the winter vacations we had, growing up. Forget Florida! Next February, I think I'm going to book a trip for Cliff and me to that Perrysburg hotel—I just checked the Internet, and they are still in business. Maybe I can even get my big brother, Davey, to join us!

33

THE DIARIES

THE STRINGS THAT HELD the old book together were barely able to secure its contents. On the left-hand side were some scribbles written by my great-grandma in German—a language I cannot decipher. I opened the tattered old diary, which seemed, at first glance, to be made out of two old postcards. But upon closer inspection, I noticed a barely-there leather material trying desperately to hold all of its possessions together, making it seem that the postcards inside were indeed the cover. One of the postcards was addressed to Mrs. Anna Kuemmel, Middle Bass Isle, Ohio. That's it. No P.O. box, no zip code. Our postmaster, J.R., would have a blast with that one!

What struck me the most was a very yellowed newspaper clipping attached to the first page with an old sewing pin. The article was titled "Bodies Stacked Found in Nazi Prison." This event, and many like them, happened in my great-grandma's home country.

Maybe this article was chosen to let future generations realize the horrific events of the past so as to never allow them to happen again. I felt a deep sense of sadness.

I could only make out half the article on the left-hand side. The other had been torn off, or over the years, had been lost to the dust that filled our old attic. Part of it read, "All of the prisoners had been sentenced for 'crime against the Reich' that had resisted the Nazis, had spoken out, perhaps the Gestapo and had declined to follow Hitler fanatically."

Wow. It made my simple life and unorganized closets seem extremely trivial.

The second page held another article, and again, this small clipping was attached using sewing pins. She must have sewn—I think every woman sewed, back then. This article was a light-hearted one about German living. Grandma Kuemmel must have also missed her home country. After visiting her home-town of Oberthalhausen, Germany, a few summers ago, I can see why she missed it. It was a small town of close-knit and loving people in which the family cemetery was right across the street from the solidly built family home. During that trip with Cliff and my sister, Natalie, I could easily see why she chose to live on Middle Bass—it was much like the small town in which she was born.

The next several pages were filled with addresses written in English. I recognized some of the family names written, but some of them were a mystery to me. Maybe they were names of people she'd met on her journey to the U.S.A. Did she send annual Christmas cards to them? Or did her diary double as an address book, too?

After all the addresses came the part of the diary I cannot read—again, because it's written in German. My family had this translated years ago, and from what I was told, it's writ-ten in an "Old German Style." I have yet to discover where I put that file on my computer, which has it typed out for me to easily understand.

As I close the book, another newspaper clipping slips out, obviously not attached by pins. It shows a picture of several men carrying a casket from what must be the Old Tin Goose airplane. As I carefully unfold the paper, I see that there are two old black and white photos on this newspaper print. Both have planes in them, one showing the scene I described above, and the other showing an old plane sitting on the edge of frozen Lake Erie with people all around. The title of this article reads, "Plane in Which Three Died Is Raised From Lake." Wow, I hadn't even heard of this story growing up—or had I?

I want to read something lighter, so I eagerly grab another diary. These books are much more solid, and the words are easily understood with Grandma Kuemmel's neatly written cursive in English. Meredith walks in and interrupts my nostalgic trip back in time.

"Mom, whatcha doing?"

She instantly takes notice of the box and books spread out across my bed, and from the smile on her face, I know she is ready to sit with me—at least for a few moments. She has heard of these special books before and of my days spent in the attic as a child rummaging through the shoebox in which they were stored. She humors me and allows me to pick up the book that contains the date that always gets me excited. I flip to it. April 24, 1973, the day I was born.

"How amazing is it that I'm holding a little book that was once held by your great-great-grandmother's hands?" I read the entry. "Tuesday, Laura Webster Put-in-Bay died 74 years old, and Linda's baby born this morning."

I was born on the same day another islander passed away. There was sadness and mourning for one family and joy for another, all in one tiny community. I feel a jolt. We are only here for a brief snippet of time. The moments we have now are just a blip on the radar of the universe.

It felt as if Grandma Kuemmel's emotions were coming

through me as I read her words in the diaries that day. Did she realize the impact she would have on me when she wrote them? What was her purpose in keeping the information tucked away inside the shoebox? Did she keep those sad newspaper clippings to teach us what *not* to do? Maybe it was just her way to pass the time and treasure it, too.

And treasure it I will, as well. Amidst all the holiday cheer, taking down the Christmas tree, and cleaning out my closet (a task I undertake every holiday) in this New Year of 2014, I'm going to resolve to be more appreciative for my amazing life, and I will try to do better. Time is ticking away as I write this, and I have so much more to do! Within each moment, I will do my best as a mom, daughter, fiancé, teacher, and business owner.

34

A WITNESS TO WINTER

IT WAS 7:00 A.M. in mid-December. I was ready for school a little earlier than normal, and so I jumped in my Honda CR-V to start my day and possibly get more grading done (grading always needs to be done!). I arrived at school with the pre-dawn darkness all around me. I fumbled through my teacher's bag, purse, and coat for my keys to the building. Darn it—no keys! I must've left them in my Smart car—the one parked in my driveway back at home. I banged on the back door where I could see another teacher already inside working, but she didn't hear me. It's no use; I would just have to go back home and watch the morning news.

Driving back the way I came, I looked up into the sky as I came to the intersection of Langram and School Road. A reddish tinge was beginning to shine through the bare branches of the distant trees. At that moment, I knew just what to do: follow the colors in the sky. This unexpected change of plans gave me the gift of a new morning island ritual. Now, each morning since the "forgotten keys incident," I spend about 15 minutes at the Bathing Beach watching the sunrise. During my times there, I have been a witness to winter like no other time in my life.

Sure, I've been out on the frozen waters of Lake Erie in my day. Like any other kid, my entire childhood, I looked forward to the first snowfall. In the past ten years, I've been to Middle Bass for delicious wings or just off for an ice adventure out to North Bass Island. But my floatsuit, once a warm, safe friend, now hangs inside my closet. It's been over two years since I've zipped myself inside the bright orange suit. And I don't really want to. I've always lived in Ohio and have had my share of winters. Now, I just want to relax into it and enjoy the feeling of it.

My CR-V was excited for this fresh, new routine as it took me to the Bathing Beach, that winter morning. I put her in park and left the heat on high, even though it was a mild 40 degrees (I like to be warm). As I zipped up my coat and opened the car door, I felt the cool air and, looking east, saw the orange-red hues begin to light up the sky, as if nature had been waiting just for me to begin the show. Walking a little farther, I could smell the familiar scent of my lake. The cry of a lone seagull flying overhead and the halyard rope banging against the flagpole at The Monument provided the soundtrack to the spectacle of color in the sky.

As I walked along the sidewalk and looked at the cracks in the seawall, my mind traveled back to a time when there was no such seawall, and the land and the lake met. Those were much simpler times for me as a young island girl. I often swam at the Bathing Beach with my summer friend, Mara Stifter. We floated on top of huge old black inner tubes and rode the waves. The bigger, the better!

Now, the Bathing Beach has changed—recently, it has been lovingly improved by some local volunteers—thank you! I know I've seen your pictures in the *Gazette*. You all have spent hours adding sand, plants, and a nice wooden walkway, complete with heavy ropes for handrails. So pretty!

But nothing compares to the colors my eyes were witnessing in that morning sky. As I breathed in the chilled air, I said my morning prayer to Mother Earth and felt the rush of nature's energy. Continuing down the sidewalk along the seawall, I gazed up at our Monument and got a little dizzy. It's so tall! I thought of naming my seagull friend but couldn't come up with anything, so I just told her out loud, "Thanks for joining me."

Realizing it was time to head back, I turned into the wind and felt the chill on my face. "It's always coming from that direction," I thought to myself, "I should've worn my scarf!" The new house next to the Bathing Beach with the extra big windows allowed the reflection of the sunrise, doubling its impact. Thank you, whoever you are, for putting in those huge windows! They have now become a looking glass for Mother Nature. Noticing the time on my watch, my Birkenstock boots picked up the pace to hurry me back to my warm car.

One more sip of my butter coffee, and I put the CR-V in drive and headed back to school. But now, as I reached the familiar building, I felt more ready than ever to help my students—to really reach them so that they could achieve their ultimate goal of learning. Deep learning. And because of this new routine of morning time with nature, I feel more connected to our island, which allows me more energy with which to do what I was meant to do here.

I don't know how long I will continue this new morning ritual, but I feel its positive ramifications already and don't think I will be letting go of it anytime soon. I will be a witness to winter and then, eventually, spring. Maybe I will even continue into the summer with her gorgeous early morning amazingness. Who knows? But for now, I will traverse the ice-covered walkways of The Monument and be always grateful for forgetting my keys that December morning.

35

I LOVE MAYFLIES

W HEN THEY LAND ALL over me while out in my gardens, I simply lift them by their wings and let them fly away. Please don't squish them. There are two reasons for this: it's not nice, and they stink when you do this. If you do try to squish them or accidentally do with your broom as you sweep them off your deck (don't say I didn't warn ya), you will smell a distinct odor of dead fish. Just love them and know they're a sign of a healthy lake and...*summertime!* I just love those mayflies.

Yes, folks, it's that time of year again! Billy Market, a.k.a. The Island Boy, who is also very talented in picture taking, posted a gorgeous picture of summer and the Miller Boats on Facebook, along with the caption, "Miller Boat Line is now on its full summer schedule!"

If I could've reached into my computer, that morning when I read that, I would've hugged The Island Boy. Instead, I hugged Cliff. And then I posted, "These are the summer days I dream of all winter!" But, I don't think Billy or the other Facebook folks really knew my excitement with that posting.

Later, boats mean comings and goings with ease for this Island Girl. But now that it's summer, I don't really want to leave! Funny how that works. But, I feel better knowing I *can* go if I please. Plus, now that the boats are running their late 9:00 PM boat from the island to the mainland, my friends living over there don't have any excuse not to visit me. *Hellooo!* You can all go back home later, Mainland Jen!

It's no socks time! This winter, I dreamt a lot about not having to put on my heavy socks, as did most people living in the Northern Hemisphere. Each morning, from about November through March, I would look out the large windows in my classroom and think of summer. I knew it was going to come—it always does—but there were mornings when I wondered if those ferry boats would ever get out of the bay again. I think even my students questioned the "four seasons" thing we've been teaching them about since they were three.

But summer did arrive on our tiny little island in Lake Erie, just as planned. Summer for us island folk means Founder's Day, celebrations at The Monument, Buffalo Man Salad at Hooligans, and so much more. This year, the June celebration of Founder's Day was a hit. I saw Trey Sheehan soaked in cold water inside the dunking tank, Barb Chrysler playing with children so lovingly, and Marissa Rence face-painting some of those same little kids. It made me think of Founder's Days past and my summer memories with friends.

When I was young, the summer cottage kids would come back, giving all us island kids such as T.J. Burgess and Libby Morrow more people to play with. Mara Stifter lived right across the street from the Dairy Queen, known today as "Dairy Isle." Her parents spoiled us and allowed us frequent trips across the street for Push-Ups, chocolate-dipped ice cream cones, and Buster Bars. Berni Isaly and her family would also arrive in the late spring to open up their West Shore cottage, and there I'd be, on the Isaly doorstep waiting to greet them. Both of these summer families had to sell their island homes, much to my disappointment, and I still miss seeing them each summer. But they both were spotted at my wedding celebration party in June! Christy Frederick, Suzanne Militello, and Kyrie Kahler were all summer girls, and they still are today. When we were young, we swam at the Crew's Nest, played softball, and celebrated summer birthdays together. Now that we're all grown up, we have cocktails at the Crew's Nest together, watch lots of softball, and enjoy seeing each other's children grow up, year after year. These family additions mean so much to our island community! I only wish they could stay all year long and suffer through—I mean—hang out with me each winter.

It was as if the cold lasted forever, and I never thought you'd come again, Summer. Thank you for arriving, even if it does mean that I must clean up stinky mayflies by spending hours with my leaf blower to rid them from my deck, house, and sidewalk. I do have to say, though, I get a great workout on my arms and wrist with all of that leaf blowing. I even get to feel some of those mayflies squish between my bare toes. [No socks!] I'm going to invent a new workout routine and call it The Mayfly Leaf Blower Workout.

Getting more exercise, watering my plants, and wearing dresses with Birkenstocks: three of my favorite things you allow me, Summer. Lake Erie boat rides, summer friends, and warmer days and nights are all things Summer. Thank you for arriving after that long and treacherous winter season. I'm loving you like never before, Summer, even those smelly little mayflies you bring along with you!

36

ISLAND DRAMA

I WAITED BACKSTAGE AND FELT the familiar feeling inside my stomach. These weren't just butterflies; there were Viking warriors inside me fighting an awful battle. I don't know why I still get such stage fright. Give me kids any day. Easy! But, adults—they're another story. Opening night had arrived, and after months of preparation, I was ready to take the stage—just as I had done so many times before as a kid here on Put-in-Bay.

As I walked through the backstage hallway, I bumped into not-so-young-anymore high school student Tatey Kowalski. "I'm so nervous!" I confessed to her. I was her first-grade teacher, and now she was seeing me in an entirely different way. She giggled and smiled at me as she patiently awaited the cue for her character to appear on stage.

Then, I walked over to Matt Tucker, a Crew's Nest employee who decided to winter here. "I'm freaking out!" I whispered in my backstage voice. He laughed at me a little and then, in full character, replied, "Calm down, Emily!" It's customary to use our stage names with one another during practices, and now, on opening night, it's a good way to stay in character and feel the moment. "Yes, Walter," I whispered back to him. One advantage of being in community theater is the opportunity to work with people you wouldn't normally come into contact with. It was great getting to know this tall "kid," who happened to be playing my husband that night.

In an attempt to calm myself, I applied more lipstick—we actors have to reapply it often. I then scolded my "son" for the night, Joseph Byrnes, as I saw him touching my highly-prized makeup brush. "Get away from there, Michael!"

I positioned myself in my favorite spot, in full sight of the main stage. Then Marc Wright, who played the impatient and funny Gimbel's store manager, appeared backstage beside me, following along with me in the script for a minute or two. Oh, he is so full of talent! Each night at rehearsal, he always made us laugh, and tonight would be no different. He was born for the stage! Sharing in my enthusiastic nervousness, we grasped our hands together with excitement.

Suddenly, I saw another high schooler—one I like to call my third daughter—Sophia Schroeder. She walked by me, showing no signs of nervousness at all. Already wearing her white doctor's coat, she was ready to make the audience laugh with a personal reference about going to the doctor.

Now, the play had begun, and I could hear Jack Booker reciting his long monologue that introduced the audience to our play, *Elf*. He didn't miss a beat, looking all gray and wrinkled, due to the talents of our makeup artists Sue Thwaite, Frankie Porsche, and Michelle LaPlante. Jack was *so* in character as old Papa Elf.

Then, appearing on the stage was Joe Fouts as Santa with all his elves: Hannah Lentz, Erin Urge, Alex Knauer, Nora Ladd, Kate Byrnes, Miyah Uszak, Olivia Christiansen, Mia Hristovski, Macy Ladd, McKenna Stacy, Max Hristovski, and Alice Lentz. After the scene, I watched as Agnes Uszak helped corral all the little ones to their places backstage, where she worked hard at keeping them occupied and quiet.

Of course, there are always behind-the-scenes people who make a play come to life. With his finger at the ready, Brian Hovey was poised to play any sound effect called for. Making sure the curtain was opened and closed at just the right times were Mike Byrnes and Matthew Stacy. When Santa's sleigh had to be moved after the elves left the stage, Brad Meyers was there to lift it, along with the help of his wife, Rachel.

This year, the local Arts Council, island community, and the island school kids all came together once again to perform. And they just didn't take on any old play...nope! They took on the enormous task of putting on an entire production. The script-writing began in the fall, with much help from Joe Fouts. Then, my daughter, Meredith Engel, and her friend and high school senior, Elliot Kowalski, headed up the organization of it all.

I could hear my almost-all-grown-up-daughter, Meredith, on stage now with Elliot, playing the lead roles, Buddy the Elf, and his love, Jovie. They worked so hard throughout all our rehearsals and organized the details months before the practices even began. Tonight was their night to shine, and as they became their characters, Elliot made everyone laugh in those green tights, elf hat, and physical antics, while Meredith amazed everyone with her a cappella singing. Both made me so proud to be a part of it all. And, I must be honest, Meredith filled my heart with so much motherly love that it can't be put into words.

Then, time seemed to speed up as I watched and listened for my cue. I followed along in my script, laughing as I watched the scene where ornery Walter sat behind his desk in New York City. "Working" along with him were Jessica Krueger, as Gina, and Kaylyn Goebel, who played Maureen.

Katherine Woishke, a member of the PIB Arts Council, also took to the stage as the cat-loving secretary of big shot, Walter.

Everyone was so "on!" The momentum of it all took over, and the audience left Put-in-Bay and fell into the story of Buddy the Elf in Manhattan.

I looked up and saw my name painted on the old brick wall above the radiator, making my nerves feel a little bit calmer. It had survived all these years. This was an old tradition among the actors of the island, but lately, it seems to have been forgotten. In the past, after participating in a play, the island kids would paint their names on one of the bricks in the old walls. Names such as Scott Market, Linda Parker (my mom), and Paul Riddle are all clearly legible. Reading those old names always gives me a sense of comfort—especially on opening night.

Gwen Market, another talented high school kid, was also waiting with me behind the stage. She must've seen the "Christie O. '88" in orange paint because she asked, "Miss Christie, how old were you in 1988?"

"I think I was a sophomore." Yes, of course I was. It had been the "Sizzlin' summer of '88," according to the old t-shirt I had from my days at the Snack House. That summer had record high temperatures and was a summer when so many changes were happening in my youth. And play practice always took me away from the pressures of my teenage years. Rehearsals each night in the off-season gave us island kids an avenue to have good, clean fun. It gave us a sense of belonging. Acting allowed us to reach within ourselves and release the drama we were all feeling but didn't know how to articulate. Oh, how I remember those nights with T.J. Burgess, Karen Goaziou, and of course Megan Faris, as she drove us all home from rehearsals in her parent's VW bus!

To become someone you're not is something that can't be explained but must be felt. It's as if it's Halloween every night on stage. After a few practices, when you least expect it, "someone else" bubbles up from inside, and you are transformed into a new person. It's an experience that takes hold, and you find yourself wanting to do it all over again and again.

Even if it takes hours of your days, weeks, and months; even if there are artistic differences amongst the crew and cast; even if Patrick Myers has to work long hours late at night to paint a beautiful Manhattan skyline with the help of his wife, Melinda; and lastly, even if you're exhausted by the end of the production—it's all worth it!

I was looking forward to the part in the show where fifth-grader Max Hristovski would play the agitated Miles Finch and jump on top of Buddy the Elf. The audience was sure to belly laugh because we had all been laughing at every single rehearsal!

My time now arrived, and I gently moved the heavy curtain out of the way, stepped on stage, and delivered my very simple first line, "Dinner's ready." Immediately, the war inside my stomach stopped, and I didn't even have to think. Suddenly I had become Emily, the mom of the show. It wasn't a big stretch from my real life, but still so fun, nonetheless.

This is the kind of drama I love. And I'm pretty sure that after seeing our play, our audience would agree with me. I think if you asked every actor who took part in this year's production, they would all smile and look back upon the time they spent on the old Town Hall stage with fondness. As long as those names can still be read on those old island bricks, drama on the island should, and will, continue. At least I sure hope so!

37

SUMMER CAMP

"WHERE IS THE TENT?" I asked the counselors when we arrived.

"Well, this camping week, so many girls signed up, we had to put you all in here," replied the head counselor. It was a long, narrow bunkhouse with about 20 bunk beds lined up along both sides of it. Kristin Altoff, my cousin Annette Luecke, and I had all decided to go to Girl Scout Camp together that summer.

My hardworking parents had paid about a trillion dollars to send me there. We were supposed to be in tents. Not a bunkhouse. Kristin had filled my mind with stories of her past experience at Girl Scout Camp, which included six girls in a tent, hangin' out, and telling ghost stories into the wee hours of the morning. This was not like the Polaroid photos she had shown me in the months leading up to our big week at Girl Scout Camp!

I was really bummin' out. My mom dropped me off, and I instantly felt the pain inside my stomach. I was already homesick the minute she was outta my sight. I can still clearly see her walking away from me that day. I was twelve—old enough to go away for a week—but felt as if I were an abandoned puppy left along the side of the road.

When we were kids, my siblings and I went camping a lot—in our backyard. I was used to that kind of camping and was so looking forward to an entire week of tenting it. Camping was so much fun! The stars at night, the smell of the wet grass in the morning, and then came the warm morning sun to dry the dew that had collected on the side of the tent during the night. Ahh!…camping! I never went to those fancy state parks or campgrounds. Instead, my backyard was my own private campground, where I loved to pitch my tent.

One night, as I lay awake, crying softly so as not to awaken the other (tougher) girls who weren't homesick, I clicked my heels together. "There's no place like home, there's no place like home," I whispered. [Really, I did this…after all, it worked for Dorothy!] I closed my eyes tightly and hoped that when I opened them, I would be back on my little island. But I wasn't. I was still inside my bunkhouse—with no tent.

The one time during the day when I wasn't homesick was when I was on my horse. My parents paid another trillion dollars to let me take riding lessons. Each day, we would go to the stables to ride horses. Kidd was my horse's name, and I loved him. Don't ask me the name of any of my counselors, because as far as I'm concerned, they were evil women who wouldn't let me go home. But, I digress…. When I got to ride Kidd, I felt exhilaration like never before. I never felt freer than when I was galloping with him. That was the best!

But then back to the bunkhouse we would go. And the night would come, along with the tears. Poor Kristin and Annette and all the other girls around us; they had to listen to my crying all week. I'm pretty sure they managed to have a great experience despite my constant crying, and I was thoroughly embarrassed at my behavior, but I couldn't help myself! I missed the lake. I missed the ferryboat horn. I missed my mom and dad. I even missed my older brother, Davey!

I tried everything I could do to get my parents to come save me from my week of pain and take me back home to my island paradise. I sent letters of desperation home, and Mom saved every one of them. I have them all inside my trunk, along with all my childhood diaries. The words are all smudged because of my tears, and on the back of one envelope, I drew an arrow pointing to one spot where a tear fell. People—I was really homesick!

Summer camp may be a good choice for some. But for this Island Girl, it was more like a prison. I prefer camping in my own backyard. Inside a tent. Even as an adult, I have camped at our State Park, right here on the island. It's beautiful, so why should I go anywhere else—right? Home. A good place for summer camp.

38

MY MOM

'VE TOLD MYSELF I won't worry. Worrying does no one any good. My mom will be fine. She's a whiz at this surgery stuff. She is holding onto hope that this surgery will help heal the many years of pain that she has had to endure in her lower back. I am hoping for the same outcome. Healing. But the long wait in the waiting room makes me worry—a little. Oh God, I'm just like my mom—a worrywart!

Then I think about the "back" itself. The back is all about support. Mom has done her fair share of supporting others her entire life. That's what mothers do, for goodness sake! They support the family, the house, the children, all while having a career.

My mom's career was the family businesses. In fact, that's where she put extra pressure on that back of hers, and it's part of the reason she is going under the knife today. Lifting heavy boxes of island freight that had just been brought over by Parker Boat Line—that didn't do her back any good at all.

Then, of course, came marriage and children, lifting each of her three children to her hip many times a day while pushing the vacuum. Not all at once, of course, but an infant every three years was challenging. In the early years of her marriage, she was also helping to raise my half-brother, Troy. A marriage, the children, and work—and tough work, at times. All of those things put a strain on her poor back.

As we boarded the plane this morning, on our way to her surgery appointment (no ferries yet), Mr. Walt Duff asked me, "You goin' too, Christie?"

I answered him sarcastically, "I gotta go with her to the hospital! Who else is gonna take care of this old lady?"

I think I shocked Mr. Duff with my comment, but not my mom. She got it. She shares my cynical humor.

But really…who else would do this? After all, I'm the daughter who lives here. I'm just down the road. Of course I'm taking her! I'm also the daughter who has had my mom right down the street, in case I needed help—for my entire life. And she has helped me with all of my heavy lifting.

During college… "Mom, can I live with you this summer so I can save my money for school?"

"Sure," she said, as she put up with my late-night social schedule for an entire summer. I tried to be quiet, Mom. Sorry.

Then, during my third year at BGSU… "Mom, I'm pregnant."

"You're going to live here," she responded and proceeded to buy a crib, sheets, diapers, and everything else that little Anna would need. She helped again when I went back to finish my undergrad degree.

About ten years later… "Mom, I'm getting divorced."

"You can stay here if you need to," she said without hesitation.

Throughout all my years as a teacher, I've given my mom many early morning calls. They would sound something like, "Mom, I've got to give my students a test today, and can't miss school. Can you take Meredith? She has a low fever but is doing better."

"Sure," always came the groggy voice on the other end of the line.

And since she always has everything needed to live, "Mom, I'm out of brown sugar. Can I borrow a cup?"

"Sure," she has replied. "Just replace it when you can buy more at the store."

My mother has been here with me through all the tough times…and all the good times, too. Christmases, Trick-or-treats, and Easter egg hunts. She was there in all those moments, and she's never left me.

Like so many mothers, mine has always been there whenever I've needed help and has always been the first one I call. She has supported my two daughters and me our whole lives. Just last week, my teenage daughter stayed at her house "just because." It's Meredith's dream to be just like my mom someday, with a house full of tissue boxes for her allergies, good cereal in the cupboard, and a great big bed in which to watch late-night movies. When Anna comes home for a visit, she knows Gramma Parker will have a bowl full of yummy stuff, and she always stops in for a handful.

I've been blessed to have my mom in my life these 41 years. Thanks, Mom. Speedy recovery to you and your newly improved back! Don't you worry; I can support myself these days. But I still may need to borrow some brown sugar (that I will promptly replace after a trip to the grocery store). Happy Mother's Day!

39

MY DAD

WHEN WE MOVED TO Lakeside, Ohio, for a few years of schooling, the mainland girls didn't know what to think of me—the Island Girl.

"Dad, the girls at school were mean to me again. We were all in the bathroom, and one of them said to me, 'Are you that girl from Put-in-Bay? What are you doing at *our* school?'"

"Who were they talkin' to—*you*? You just tell them that your dad will come and have a talkin' to them! Tell them your family is from Marblehead, and I know their fathers!"

"No, Dad! That would embarrass me!"

Then he would imitate them, talking as if he were a teenage girl (it was the 80's and the Valley Girl talk had just begun). "So—like Christie Ontko—like gag me with a pitchfork—she is—like—from that *island!*"

This would make me smile. Then, in my pre-teen girl emotional state, I would cry, and he would bring me to his lap and allow me to sob. Those years were the toughest years of my life. Adolescence.

My dad was always patient with me during that time and, as I continued to grow up, I continued to mess up. But he was still calm with me about my decisions in life. I could tell when he disapproved of the things I did. For instance, when I dated not-so-perfect boys. He was always nice to them and always had a smile when they were around. But I knew my dad and could tell when he didn't approve.

He always allowed me to make my own mistakes and was there to shower me with love and compassion when the realization of my errors hit me. Never did he give me the "I told you so" talk. He really didn't like any of them—those boys, that is. [Come to think of it, as I look back and cringe, I can easily see why.]

I quickly learned after having a baby while still being in college that I needed a car. My dad helped me buy my first automobile and loaned me the cash to purchase it. When I began making money as a teacher, I went to him with pride, offering to repay the loan.

"Keep it," he said. "You finished school, and I'm so, so proud of you."

My dad. The man I called one late night in tears when my colicky second-born daughter, Meredith, wouldn't let me sleep. Even though he had to work the next day at Miller Boat Line, he arrived quickly (he was still living on the island then), and we all piled into his car for the two-minute drive to his house. Anna, then four years old, little Meredith, screaming all the way, and me. I got my first solid night of sleep that summer evening, all because of my dad.

"Dad, you've got a noodle on your chin," I alerted him as he was slurping up his soup recently.

"I'm saving it for later," he quickly replied.

That's my dad. Always making a joke. I wanted to reach across the table and wipe it off myself. "Dad, seriously, you look like a bum, wipe it off, already!" I said with laughter. He is a 75-year-old man today, but to me, he's still my young dad with a loving, old soul.

He giggles, wipes his chin, and without missing a beat, tells me another detail about his toy trains in the garage on Catawba at The Vineyard.

Dad, hopefully, things will slow down in my life soon, and I can visit you and those trains again or take you out for another bowl of soup at Big Boy. Please know that I'm okay now and don't need too much more "fixing" (I hope). But, if someone is mean to me at school, I know that you will always be there to let me climb up on your lap and cry.

Happy Father's Day to you—Charlie/Chuck/Tuna Ontko.

40

YARD FUN

Y EARS AGO, CLIFF WAS cursing the rocks in our yard, but
I knew it would only be a matter of time before he would
embrace them. Those rocks now line most of the gardens
at our home on Thompson Road. The shades of gray and the
unique shapes of the rocks separate the green grass from all the
hostas, roses, and other perennials. We have even moved some
of our precious rocks from Thompson Road to the Freshwater
Retreat house on Langram Road. Those rocks are like diamonds
to me because they add so much beauty to the landscape.

Yard work is something that I guess you could say is in
my genes. The Parkers of Put-in-Bay have been known for
their amazing yards and gardens. Just drive by Aunt Jeanette
Luecke's house. Wow! How do she and my Uncle Tim have time
for all that? [Especially with their love of holding garage sales.]
My late Uncle Joe Parker also comes to mind when thinking of astonishing gardens. Today I get to watch his daughter, Marsha Parker, running around in her golf cart taking
care of so many island gardens. Cousin D.J. is busy growing
grapevines above the large arbor at his ice cream place. My
relatives have the ability to grow things so beautifully that it
must be genetically linked back to England, where the name

REFLECTIONS OF AN ISLAND GIRL

Parker actually means "keeper of the Park."

When I was a little girl, I would observe my mom in her gardens that surrounded our house. She grew many flowers from seed, and watching her perennials pop up every spring was something she looked forward to. Each year in late April, right around the time of my birthday, my mother would point out the Dutchman's Breeches wildflowers in the woods across the street from our house. She would be so happy to see a sign of spring after the long winter, and I am the same way. My mom taught me about flowers and gardening through her example.

I learned how to pick the seeds from such annuals as marigolds and then save them in brown bags for the following year. I would watch her tomato plants grow tall and eat those delicious red fruits with a fresh egg on bread. Pure yum. When the screams would come, as they always did, I knew my mom had encountered a toad or snake in her gardens. Today, she still works hard out there in her yard. Now, she has a small menagerie of garden toys and welcoming signs near the side entrance to her house. As you walk underneath her arbor, depending upon the holiday, you'd be likely to hear Christmas bells or perhaps a witch's cackle at Halloween.

The three Ontko children weren't allowed to play in Mom's flowerbeds. No dirt for us. Instead, Davey, Natalie, and I got the job of cleanup. Collecting all the weeds that were stacked in piles all around the house was our job. There we'd be, moaning and complaining as we picked them up and hauled them away with our old blue wheelbarrow. Crossing the street to Grandpa Parker's woods, we would dump them and then pile little Natalie back inside the empty wheelbarrow, pushing her back to the house for another load.

Then came those pesky walnuts. Oh, how I hated those things! [I still do!] We kids were in charge of cleaning those up, too, so they wouldn't break the lawnmower. We'd make a game out of it as we tossed them into the wheelbarrow. Thunk. Thunk. Thunk. Then my brother Davey would get carried away and begin "missing" and accidentally hit Natalie or me. Oh, the walnut wars we had!

Looking back, it seems that yard work wasn't all that bad, but when I was a kid, I hated it! Now, I love the work of the yards. I think I'm going to call it Yard Fun from now on. Yard Fun gives you an amazing suntan. Yard Fun makes you move your body after the long Put-in-Bay winter. It's so freeing to plant things and then decide a year later that you want it elsewhere. With the help of the Put-in-Bay Garden Club, last year, I was taught where certain plants should be and that it's "okay" to get rid of plants that are overgrown or not fitting in the garden anymore. I was so relieved to learn the great tips from those garden geniuses. They love Yard Fun, too!

One day, I hope to earn the title of "Master Gardener," like the amazing garden queen, Carol Root. In the meantime, I will pretend I'm a garden princess. It's so gratifying to plant rose bushes and then watch as each bud appears, flowering into the most beautiful vision and delightful smell ever. Popping a freshly picked cherry tomato into my mouth or cutting my lavender and then using it to make my homemade balm is just so very cool. Choosing to weed one day, plant on another, and lay fresh mulch in a newly created garden makes me feel so grown up and "in charge." I love to stand back and adore my little spaces of growth. And, if you take a ride around the island at this time of year, you will marvel at all the gardens of so many talented—and very tan— island folks.

Recently, Cliff and I decided to plant four small grape-vines. With the expertise and help from Mr. Walt Duff, we are expecting delicious Niagara grapes in the next several years.

We're planning to plant Concord, too. Maybe I will learn how to make APW (Alfred Parker Wine) that was made famous by Grandpa Alfred Parker so many years ago. You never know how far I will take this garden fun stuff. It's just in my genes!

41

TEST YOUR ISLANDER-NESS II

SOME OF YOU TOOK last year's test very seriously, and I thank you for that. I spent hours grading all your tests last March. The following is an updated version of the Islander-ness test—with a spin. This one will test your age *and* your Islander-ness. Since I will be "over the hill" in late April, I thought it fitting.

This test has been calibrated by The Islanders Test Commission Group, who have humbly asked to remain anonymous. These questions have been tested and retested by current and former islanders of age 40 and older. If you have any questions regarding the questions, scoring, or validity of this test, please contact Gordon Barr, the President of the Islanders Test Commission Group.

Answer the following questions with this point system:

2 = yes
1 = maybe/sometimes
0 = definitely *not*!

1. Do you recall when there was a large open pit in front of the Put-in-Bay grocery store? Or, do you recall when there was *no* grocery store?

2. Did you attend the school when there were at least three grades per classroom?

3. Are you tired of explaining the answer to the question, "What's it like during the winter?"

4. When younger, was your idea of a winter vacation going to the mainland? (Please refer to *Chapter 32: Winter Break* for further clarification.)

5. Have you ever eaten grapes off the vine until your stomach hurts?

6. Have you worked at least ten years of summer jobs doing work such as: cleaning rooms, waiting tables, bartending, washing dishes, lifeguarding, and/or working in retail? Give yourself a bonus point if you've done *all* these jobs.

7. Can you remember the time where the last boat on White Spider Night was *truly* the end of the season?

8. Did you graduate from any of the island schools on or before 1991?

9. Have you ever played a video game in the arcade with purple carpeting at The Colonial?

10. Can you remember the old Victorian homes where the new Monument Visitor Center now stands?

11. Do you recall the night when The Castle burned down?

12. Have you ever gone through The Haunted Forest on Shady Path?

13. Do you remember when Joe Parker would fill your car up with gas at the garage? *And* clean your windows?

14. Can you recall the time when tourists would randomly find their way into the school? [We'd be sitting there in class,

and all of a sudden, a person with a camera around his neck would be wandering through the hallways.]

15. Lastly, do you recall when island phone numbers were only four or fewer digits? And we had party lines!

26-30: **OVER THE HILL!**
According to Debbie Bianchi, the age of 40+ is simply awesome. Whoo-hoo! You made it!!! You've earned this age and don't be afraid to tell the whole island how old you are! Be proud!

18-25: **SORTA OLD**
In a few years, you'll get to be over the hill, too. Or, maybe you never played Pac-Man while asking Jeff Niese for quarters. Perhaps, you were a chicken and stayed home during Halloween instead of seeing The Girl Scouts all dressed up in scary costumes on Shady Path.

0-17: **SUPER YOUNG**
You probably don't know what a camera on a string is, let alone recall the day when the school was left unlocked throughout the day. "What was The Castle?" you may ask. You've never dialed only a 4-digit number to reach someone and probably can't work a rotary phone. Party line? Is that something where everyone stands in a line, and then the party starts? Wow…you are young. But don't worry; you'll get there. We all do.

42

PARTY LIKE AN ISLANDER

A FTER A HARD SUMMER filled with hours of long working days, it was as if the whole island had gotten together for a family reunion—minus all the family drama. Everywhere you turned, there was a familiar face. Not just locals, either. Visitors who love the island and visit often were also in attendance. Past summer employees, former islanders, and friends were all around! People who hadn't seen each other all summer due to busy schedules got to catch up. I even got to see my mom and my daughter—all on the *same* night! All the fun and laughter experienced was because of one woman and her family. You see, Katrina Spatafore found out she has breast cancer. Katrina, even though a private woman, is a most-loved and adored Island Girl. Her dear friends, Billy and Allie Market, decided to organize a fund-raising event in an effort to help with all the added expenses of conquering this illness. Reel Bar and The Forge also pitched in, along with local musicians who volunteered their talents for an evening of island fun.

It began inside The Forge with food, prizes, and people. Raffle tickets were purchased, and along with everyone else, Cliff and I started dropping ours into the red Round House buckets beside each prize, hoping to win its contents. Items such as a gorgeous geode from Mr. Kindt's rock collection, a telescope from Anne and Pat Dailey, and cookies made by June Stoiber were all a part of the raffle. Merchandise from local gift shops and island businesses were also available prizes. There was even some kind of raffle going on for a golf cart—I'm serious! A golf cart! Sadly, I didn't get in on that one quickly enough, and the tickets had sold out before I knew it! Kim Morrison won the scooter being raffled off, and I knew this because her hubby, Skip, ordered a fancy bottle of wine (or was it champagne?) to celebrate her win—and forgot to offer Cliff and me a glass! One of my favorite items being raffled off was ice cream every week for the entire summer of 2019 from The Candy Bar. *And guess who won it?* Me!! So many people generously donated, allowing wishes to come true for many in attendance.

Next, the party continued over at The Reel Bar, where some serious excitement took place. A real live auction! How exciting! The auction began with Billy Market behind a microphone on the stage. I gotta say he did an *amazing* job of keeping the party moving. I witnessed others helping him, too: daughter, Caiti, and her mom, Jane, along with Round House Paula and Ashley, just to name a few. Cliff and I took a seat at the family table of the Market clan. Anytime I can, I love to sit with them because they're *hil-ar-ious!* Julene + Scott beside one another = funny.

I heard about an old Parker Boat sign that was to be auctioned off. [Alfred Parker was my grandpa who owned Parker Boat Line, where the *Jet Xpress* is now.] Then, just to get my facts straight, I walked over to Bob Stausmire for information. He had worked for my grandpa, and I knew he'd know about this mystery sign. As it turned out, it was from the side of the boat named *The Yankee Clipper*, and Bob knew this because he was the one who had made the sign! In those days, they were hand-painted on a wooden board and attached to the side of the ferry.

My cousin Debby Parker took a seat behind me, and we discussed our strategy for getting that sign. We agreed that Debby should get it (because she had more money to bid than I). The bidding began, and Debby put her hand up. There's nothing like an island auction to get your blood pumping, your adrenaline rushing, and your senses on high-alert. It's like chocolate! We did our best to help Debby win that sign, but another island collector bid more. Oh well—there was more to bid on: a guitar signed by Pat Dailey, a fishing trip on a fancy boat in Costa Rica, a private party at Jack and Lorain's house, and lots more! With each item being auctioned off, you could feel the generosity of the island people. We all knew that with every transaction, Katrina, Duff, and their two gorgeous young daughters would benefit from our fun that night.

Billy said it beautifully, "We can't take away your cancer, but we can help to lighten your load."

There was no sadness that night—only a feeling of giving, giving, and more giving, along with lots of laughter. Cancer is no fun. I have witnessed this disease in too many friends and too many family members. And I gotta believe that we're already on the road to beating this illness because of all the goodness and love I felt that night on this tiny little island in Lake Erie. Because, folks, we islanders know how to party!

43

SEEING THE RAINBOWS

THIRTY-TWO YEARS. THAT'S HOW long it took this Island Girl to make a trip to North Bass Island. Just ask Michele Heineman about it, because she was my witness that cold winter day, ten years ago. I'm not sure why I never went there with my old high school pal, Jennifer Burris, who grew up on North Bass. Why hadn't I ever visited the vast acres of beautiful grapes and that little one-room schoolhouse? I suppose life was just too busy for my family and me on Put-in-Bay during those days. What about the time beyond high school? Busy still, I guess.

Now, at forty-two years of age, I was about to experience even more island fun that—shame on me—I should've witnessed many years before.

As I was walking home from school the other day, attempting to get a little fall exercise in, I noticed the winery guys immersed in their relaxed, yet busy, winemaking day. I waved and gave a shout-out to Daniel Sexton, "How was your day?"

"Great!" he replied as he waved back, continuing to clean the large empty barrels.

This little guy—not so little anymore—was in my arms when he was just days old. The baby of my childhood friend, Libby

Morrow, I was around little Daniel a *lot*. When he was two years old, he enjoyed rummaging through my purse and still loves it when I remind him of this. He was always inquisitive and very well behaved. I'm sure Eddie Heineman and the rest of the winery crew are glad to have him as part of their team!

"You guys look like you're always having so much fun!" I holler back with a smile and continue, "Can I come work there for a day, and you go teach my class?"

Then I see the boss come out of the shadows. The infamous Island Wine God, Ed Heineman. [I still call him Eddie, but I think it's "Ed," nowadays.]

"Hey, your sister was just here, and she was asking when we were pressing again so Cassie can come to watch."

Natalie, my little sister, is living on the island for one year while her husband is deployed in Afghanistan and Iraq. Her two children are enrolled in our school, and, as they are in a military family, the girls are used to new experiences and moving around. I think they're extra happy to be home and around family this year. My sister is an awesome mom and is great at organizing activities and experiences for her kids. Skiing in the Swiss Alps, weekend trips to Paris, and life in the South are just a few of the adventures she has taken Vivian and Cassie on. And now, here she was organizing a fall island event to take her youngest to something that I've walked or driven past hundreds of times—an island experience I've simply taken for granted—pressing grapes.

Heck, I hadn't even *thought* of watching grapes be pressed as an "experience." But—*hello!*—it totally is. I am having downright mom guilt now. Have Anna and Meredith ever seen grapes from the Duff Vineyards get made into delicious wine and grape juice? Huh?? I don't think so. Heck, come to think of it, have *I* ever seen this process?

Stopped now on the side of the road, I don't know if Ed is telling me about my sister and Cassie coming, just to share island information, or perhaps giving me an invitation to come, too? I decide it's an invitation and I say, "I think I'll join you!" and I wave good-bye to the winery workers.

I call Natalie and ask her if it's okay if I come along, too. "Of course!" she responds. "Cassie loves having her 'Aunt T.T.' around." I smile to myself, hearing the childhood name Natalie called me since she was unable to pronounce "Christie." Now it's what Cassie calls me. Practically jogging home in my teacher's clothing, I trot down the street, grab the dog from our neighbor, "Ma Werty," and then run into the house like a little kid. I quickly change into a comfortable pair of jeans while I wait for Natalie to text me, letting me know when it's time.

After about twenty minutes, I see a message on my iPhone that reads, "It's going down!"

As I pass the Shady Path entrance on the way to the wine pressing, my grandpa Alfred Parker comes to mind. He used to make his own wine. "APW," they called it: "Alfred Parker Wine." Grandpa has been gone a long, long time, but if he were still here today, he would say to me, "What ya mean you've never seen this before? You call yourself an "Island Girl?" Why… goddammit, that paper should take away that title of yours!" I smile as I can see him in his carefully-ironed white captain's shirt, steering the *Erie Isle*.

I get to the winery just in time for the action, walk over to my sister and give my cutie-pie niece a hug. The grapes are being poured into a huge stainless steel funnel that does something special to the fruit. From there, they are vacuumed through a large, thick hose and then are put into the press. Very cool. The press starts to hum loudly as it is activated. I watch the delicious juice pour into a basin underneath.

The smell is simply intoxicating (pun intended).

My mom arrives, and Ed treats us all to a little glass of wine (or two) from a bottle he opens. It's my favorite: Cedar Woods Red. Soon, Ed's beautiful wife Michele shows up. These days, our families keep us so busy we don't see each other like we used to. We laugh as we reminisce about that winter trip to North Bass Island and another day trip we took there with Michele's dad, John Dodge, and my mom, Linda Parker.

We all follow Ed into the large barns as he teaches us about the winemaking process and the science behind it all. I hope he is teaching somebody all this stuff because it's quite a bit to remember! So much sugar here, watching the yeast growth there, the white grapes are treated differently than the red ones…wow, it's a lot!

Looking healthier than ever, Mr. Kindt arrives with his daughter Vicki, his kind wife, and their little dog, all on the island golf cart. They've come to enjoy Ed's company, so my family and I decide it's time to take off for home.

As I walk down the winery road back to my house, I am feeling grateful for my island life and little sister, Natalie. Little does she know the impact she's had on me by moving back home. Not only do I get to see my two nieces every day in school and see them every holiday this entire year, but Natalie has also taught me about the importance of being home. She has helped to remind me that I'm sometimes too busy, and I take this precious island and all her amazing experiences for granted. Just as those living in Hawaii might not see the rainbows anymore, those of us living here may not be seeing the great island experiences all around us each season.

44

ONLY ON AN ISLAND

I T WAS THE DAY before my youngest child Meredith was leaving for college, and she still hadn't yet received her laptop from Apple.

"Wait! I think I got an email saying that it was delivered to the post office; let's go check with J.R. later when the window opens up again," I suggested. Meredith agreed and continued packing up her bedroom.

On the island, the delivery of items isn't as easy as it is on the mainland. No fancy post office man comes to your mailbox while your dog barks like crazy. UPS workers dressed in all brown outfits never leave boxes outside our front doors. We island folk just accept this, are used to it, and take it with a very relaxed approach.

Usually.

Getting this computer was critical to my already nervous girl, as she was packing up her belongings and getting ready for the next step in her early adult life. This computer would hold hundreds of college papers, calculus equations, and maybe even her future résumé. She needed that new MacBook!

The clock turned to 2:00 pm, the time that the Post Office window re-opens after their lunch break. So, in the Smart car we went. But only going the speed limit of 25, I swear.

Walking eagerly past the glass doors and saying our usual hellos to our island friends and relatives, I waltzed over to the window with confidence, reassuring Meredith that J.R. would indeed have her new computer.

"I don't see anything here," J.R. said.

Uh oh.

Using my handy smartphone, I rechecked my email, and when I read more slowly, I realized my mistake. "Oh, J.R., I'm so sorry; it says UPS, *not* USPS!"

He gave me a kind and patient grin, as I'm sure he has heard this story many, many times in his tenure behind the island post office counter.

In the meantime, a text came through from my hubby, Cliff, saying, "Bob Gatewood picked up our boxes. He put them on the table."

I shared this information with both my daughter and J.R., and he quickly offered to help. "Bob is playing now at the Round House, do you want me to call him and leave a voicemail?"

"Nah, we will figure this out," Meredith told him. "Thanks, J.R.!"

We got back into our tiny island car and jetted back to our house, eager to find the box which held this expensive item. No computer box or packages anywhere. We looked on the kitchen table, the kitchen counter, and the outdoor table on the porch. Nothing.

So, a trip to Miller Boat Line was in order. Maybe Bob took our packages back to the boat dock? Maybe on a table there? In the meantime, I tried calling Cliff. No answer, as he was probably baiting someone's hook during one of his fishing charters.

Meredith and I would figure this mystery out on our own. One last bonding experience before college.

Miller Boat Line didn't have our packages. They confirmed to us that Bob did indeed take our stuff by mistake. Gatewood, under "G," is right next to "F," where packages for Freshwater Retreat are held. No biggie. We understood, but we also wanted to find that computer. So, to the Round House we went.

When we got there, Meredith and I saw the tourists jamming to Bob's beat and knew the bouncer wouldn't let my 18-year-old inside. We attempted to explain our dilemma to him, but of course, he did his job well, and Meredith waited at the back door outside as I went in.

I squirmed through the hot tourists, made my way to the middle of the curved bar, and waited patiently as Bob finished his song. Then, when I heard the last strum on his guitar strings, I hollered to him.

"Bob! Hey, Bob!" I called.

Nothing. He had no idea I was trying to call his name but instead flashed the audience his gorgeous musician smile. Then, a nice, taller man next to me waved his hand and got Bob's attention for me.

Bob saw me, and before I had time to say anything, he shouted over the bartenders, "Hey Christie! I left your boxes on the table at your house!"

"Where?" I asked, shouting back.

Then, before I knew what was happening, the packages and I became part of the afternoon show. Bob quickly switched back into entertainer mode.

"Hey, everyone! Only on an island would this happen. I accidentally took this young lady's boxes from the delivery area on the island at the Miller Boat." The audience got quieter as he continued, "And...I accidentally opened a few of them..." the audience waited a bit longer... "You should *see* what she orders online!"

Laughter erupted from the beer-holding tourists as Bob played to the audience with humor. I enjoyed it, too.

We found the computer, and a few other packages, on a table around the side of the house, where my guests enter the retreat—a table that neither of us had checked. Silly us.

As we left the Round House with the audience cheering us along, I noticed that Meredith was wearing an uncomfortable smile.

"Mom, the bouncer just asked me out."

45

ISLAND DOG

M Y DOG, FAIR, TURNED 15 recently, and it dawned on me that she's been around longer than my husband, Cliff! This Australian Shepard/Cocker Spaniel mix is very friendly, and in spite of her vicious bark at passersby, when I lived at the old Nissen House downtown, she was a very nice and loving dog. Always at my side in the kitchen, sleeping next to me each night, and protective when I need her to be, she has been my constant companion all these years.

But, she doesn't like to stay home. She likes to roam the island and visit everyone and every place. She has even been known to make it into the Island General Store, especially in the off-season. Fair knows all about those automatic doors and would just walk on in like a human!

She likes to walk up and down Thompson Road, slowing all the cars down considerably, since they'd have to brake to avoid a collision (which, I personally think is a *great* way to slow everyone down!). Fair always acts like nothing has happened at the near misses and just saunters off the road with tail wagging and tongue hanging out. I've seen her nearly hit about a hundred times. Each time I call her, but she pretty much ignores me, enjoying the near misses, I think. Whenever the traffic comes near my wandering dog, I close my eyes and pray she gets out of their way. And thankfully, she always does. I have tried the fences. The electric kind worked instantly with Fair because she is super brilliant and a very gifted dog that learns quickly (not that I am a biased dog mommy or anything). One little high-pitched beeping sound warns her to stay away from the road before a shock is emitted from her specially-equipped collar. It only took once for her to remember, each spring. But she had also learned to test it. If the collar was too loose or batteries were low—she would run. Unfortunately, we had to stop using the collar because of a bad rash it gave her. So, no more electric fence—and that means a wandering dog, once again. [Anyone need an electric fence monitor with collar, no wires necessary?]

I had always assumed that my meandering dog bothered my neighbors, until one day, as I was on my usual after-school perusing of Facebook, I noticed my dog in several pictures of the news feed, and I wasn't the one who had posted them! Here is what my neighbor, Joan Wertenbach wrote:

> "Toda, I was heading to make my usual stops. I got to the corner, looked in my rearview mirror, and saw Fair running as fast as she could. I didn't want her to run all the way downtown, so I got out, rolled down the window, and opened the passenger side door for her. We went to the garage, then on to get gas, to the post office, the Bay Shore Resort store, State Park, Lime Kiln, and then home. She enjoyed her ride so much that she didn't want me to leave."

Well, now I finally know what my dog does when I'm at school all day! Joan Wertenbach, or as the islanders lovingly call her "Ma Werty," often feeds Fair scraps and gives her lots of love whenever Fair wanders across the road for a visit. Ma truly loves that dog, even though Fair also enjoys chasing her cats!

When I work in my shop, I often bring Fair with me. She loves to greet all the tourists and gets lots of attention from them. But she can't sit still for long, so off she will go to visit Steve at the Bird's Nest. [My cat, Charlie, often visits Steve, too.]

Isn't it great to live in such a small community where the neighbor dog is known by name? And isn't it amazingly cute when I'm gone all day and my dog is out, that she even gets her own private tour of the island with Ma Werty? I am sure some of the neighbors might not be as fond of Fair, and I have to admit that she frustrates me to no end when she runs and won't listen to me. But instead of being angry with her, I have chosen to let my old dog be happy. She won't be with us too much longer, and each time she runs to Ma's house or scurries around at the Bird's Nest, I know she will always come back with a big dog smile on her face, having enjoyed another day of adventure.

46

HATS

D O YOU EVER FEEL frustrated? I do. I'm trying to tell my fingers to stop. Stop the typing right *now*! But they have a mind of their own.

You see, folks, this month is test month at our amazing little island school. Test month. How does that sound to you?

I may get some backlash about this, but I feel it must be written about, spoken about, and discussed so that changes can occur.

As per our staff meeting yesterday, I was informed that our students are participating in the newest brand of Ohio-mandated testing called PARCC tests. These aren't your average fill-in-the-bubble tests, but they're oh, so much more!

I was confident in my students' abilities to pass these tests when first told about them. I was sure, partially because of their remarkable technological abilities on those machines called computers.

I remain confident in my students' abilities to perform well. They will grow up, and I hope some will stay on our little island and continue to build on what we've taught them. Some will move on from here and then return home seasonally to the comforts of family, local potlucks, and a lot of hard work.

Others will go off to greener pastures and live and work all over the world.

I can't predict who will do what—that is up to each one of the many kids I've had the honor of teaching. What I *can* predict, however, is that their level of success cannot and will never be determined by this series of tests.

Two people on this Earth call me "Mom." Others call me by my nickname, "Christie," and for the many children I've taught over the past 18 years, I'm known as "Miss Christie." We all wear different hats, living here, don't we? Sometimes, these hats aren't ever really taken off. I know a mom's hat is on all the time. For instance, even though my girls are almost all grown up, my cell phone is nearby at all times in case of an emergency phone call or text from one of them.

In the depths of these island winters, I've worn the "Miss Christie" hat. Late at night, when I'm in bed, my head is thinking about the lessons I've got to teach the next day. Or when in line at the grocery store, I may have a parent ask me about the homework I'd assigned that afternoon. I used to attempt to tell people that after 3:00, I'm no longer Miss Christie, but this simply didn't work. To many, that's who I will always be. And I'm very proud of the work she has done, the children she has loved, and the lessons she has agonized over.

But, it's time to hang up that hat. It's time for "Miss Christie" to use her creativity and energies for other adventures. I'm not sure what hat will be worn next, but I do know when it's time to change. I know that this educational system no longer fits my teaching style, and I can no longer sit idly by, watching it deteriorate. There are many things still good about public education, but there is much to be improved upon, as far as I am concerned, and I no longer have the energy or stamina to constantly fight it all. I am not a fighter. I'm a peacemaker and lover. Children—I will always love them—and hopefully, in the future, our Washington folks will get a clue. A big one. Until then, I will allow this desk to be occupied by some newer, younger energy. I wish the new teacher a fabulous time with these island children. They are so special; they are not only the future leaders of our island, but that of the state of Ohio, the country, and the world!

47

THE NEWBIES GUIDE TO ISLAND LIFE

#1: DO *NOT* TALK about others in a negative way. It's true, folks; many islanders are connected to one another. But, contrary to popular belief, we are not *all* related. For instance, I am not really "related" to—let's say, Libby (Morrow) Miller. But, as far as I'm concerned, since I grew up with her, she is like a sister to me. So don't go slamming *anyone* in her family because I just might bite your head off. [Only I can talk badly about any of them because I've known them my whole life. That's the special exception clause in rule #1.]

#2: Get your potluck dish ready. Make it yummy, too. Actually, you may need a few dishes.

#3: Don't send a drink back to the bartender because it isn't to your liking. Just drink it, silly! Don't complain! [My well-meaning and loving husband Cliff did this when he first arrived…I was *so* embarrassed.]

#4: Don't describe to others what it's like to grow up here when you just moved here four years ago. [Cliff, hint hint…]

#5: Don't get involved in every volunteer group and try to change everything. Just because you have an idea from your perspective (even though it's a *great* idea)—don't be too quick to announce it. Be patient with the islanders. They'll come around—but in their own time. Islanders love you and want your ideas, but you must be patient, not pushy.

#6: Don't leave your ice shanty on the frozen lake for the *whole* winter—despite your wife and your friends and everyone around you suggesting you should, perhaps, move it. If you don't move it, it may just float away towards Canada in the spring. [Ask Cliff about how to move an ice shanty.]

#7: Don't wait until the last boat to gather your winter supply of canned goods. Instead, start stocking up in July. My hint is, when you go shopping, place three of each thing you like in your grocery cart. For instance, if your family loves applesauce, place three of them in your cart *every time* you go to the mainland for groceries. If you begin this process in July and do it every week or so, you will be good when it's wintertime. [Call my mom, Linda Parker, for more "Winter Stock-Up Tips." She is the pro.]

#8: Be prepared to take in a stray. This could be a cat, a dog, or even a human. You see, when you live on an island, it's up to all of us to take care of them.

#9: Remember, you are a *Newbie*. You should just listen, watch, and follow the lead of an experienced islander. Even I don't know everything about living here, and I've done it my whole life! I constantly have to check with my mom about correct island etiquette.

#10: Be nice. Be kind. Contribute. Give back to the community. Now that you live here, you must help make this the best place ever! Welcome to island life.

48

CHRISTIE'S FAVORITE THINGS

THAT SAVVY BUSINESS LADY, Oprah, is truly one of my heroines both in matters of business and living a spiritual life. Now, you can get all of her "favorite things" for Christmas directly from AMAZON.COM. Well, since I'm all about sticking to "local first" when it comes to gift-giving, I have some great ideas for those of you who may be stuck and not know what to get that special someone this year for the holidays. And, unlike Oprah and the 93 things she shares with her readers, I'm sticking with ten awesome things to share with you. Otherwise, Jeff would have to print a whole additional *Gazette* just for my column! Lastly, for the record, I wasn't given any money or anything for endorsing the following products. Well, except for the last one….

ANYTHING JEWELRY

Found at The Little Store, there is so much to choose from. With prices averaging about $22.00, you're sure to find the right gift. I walked in this summer and saw Pam, who helped in the ordering of all that beautiful stuff, and I was nearly blown over. *So* many choices of colors, styles, and designs. FYI, most girls I know love the bling.

A PASS ON A FERRYBOAT

Check out MILLERFERRY.COM—for only $385.00* you can get on that boat anytime you want from Put-in-Bay, or for $65.00 more, you can include Middle Bass! Just think of all the rides your loved one can take. Buy them before Jan. 1 for the best price. Or, go to JET-EXPRESS.COM. Now, I couldn't find a season pass to buy, but instead found the "Crew Perks Card," which makes you a VIP JetSetter! Sign someone up for this special VIP card by texting "jetsetter" to 22828 and follow the prompts. [I did it because who doesn't want to be a very important person and ride that really fast boat?]

SALAD WITH BREADED CHICKEN

With a gift certificate to Tipper's Restaurant, you can get this yummy salad right after all that holiday ham. And, it's priced at under $15.00, even if you include a pop. Sandy and Patty are both so wonderful, and they will make sure your salad is extra yummy. If you ask, and tip well, they will put hot sauce on the side, and then you can dip your chicken in it. Ask for the best Blue Cheese dressing on the island. The salad hits the spot when you want to eat healthy with a salad but still want a little bit of fried Christmas naughtiness.

HEAVY-DUTY WELCOME MAT

Found at The Island Hardware Store, these wondrous doormats are not only durable and exceptional at grabbing the garden dirt, but they are so pretty, too! [They're made out of rope. I wonder if Jason and Chris sit in the back and make these things themselves?] I've had mine for at least two years! At $59.99 each, you could get two and keep one for yourself. You won't be sorry, and your loved one will have cleaner floors. Remember that all the little stores next to

Island Hardware, in our Island Outdoor Mall, will be open this holiday season!

AN AIRPLANE RIDE

If you go to FLYGRIFFING.COM or ISLANDAIRTAXI.COM, you will find out so many things about flying! Griffing has lots of planes, and they can even fly you out of the country to Pelee Island, but make sure you have a passport handy. For only $46.75, you can fly one way to any United States Lake Erie Island from Port Clinton, Ohio. *And*, to my cat-loving friends: kitties are no extra charge! Very cool. Dustin Schaffer runs Island Air Taxi, but my phone lists him as "Dusty the Plane Guy." Call or text him at (419) 573-2960 to schedule your flight to the U.S. Lake Erie Islands for $40.00 one-way. He also sells a ticket booklet for $400.00 for 11 flights. I am pretty sure cats are free with him, too. Meow!

ISLAND RESTAURANT GIFT CERTIFICATE

Cameo Pizza, The Old Forge, Hooligans, Mossbacks, The Boardwalk, The Goat, The Brewery, or Pasquales—I can honestly say I've eaten at all of these places, and each has its own flair and special dish. If you contact me on my website at FRESHWATERRETREAT.COM, I can get you in touch with one of the above owners and help you get this stocking stuffer gift certificate. At least, I think I can.

BEN AND JERRY'S TOFFEE COFFEE ICE CREAM

Purchased easily at The Island General Store, this little tub of deliciousness is only $5.25. Just make sure you keep it in the freezer until *right* before you wrap and give it as a gift. And, maybe add a spoon purchased from the Resale Shop. Last time I checked, they had at least ten spoons in various designs and flexibility.

HOMEMADE SOUPS

Topsy Turvey's. I love soup—who doesn't? After a cold snowmobile ride on the ice, this will warm your body, heart, and soul. Get a gift certificate for your honey, and maybe put enough value on it to include a mixed beverage drink—$20.00 should be enough, but don't forget to tip the bartender!

PASTA

During the winter, it's okay to eat carbs. You're hiding that tummy underneath a big warm sweater anyway. The Reel Bar hosts pasta night on Thursdays. I went last week, and it was pure yummy. You get a little card—kind of like a sushi place—and you get to choose what you want on your pasta by checking off items listed on the card. The best part? You can order gluten-free! Get a gift certificate for this place, and at Christmas, your family will be dreaming of pasta instead of sugarplums.

LAVENDER BALM

Buy this great-smelling and healing product in little recyclable jars from Freshwater Remedies. Sm. $7.95/Lg. $14.95 I make this balm in my own little island kitchen, infusing lavender from my own gardens. True story. And, I *love* it. Evidently, so do many others! I've sold so much of this stuff that I've had to plant a dozen more lavender plants to keep up with demand. Use it to soothe dry/itchy skin, baby's bottoms, hands, and cuticles. It also works well to heal burns. Try it. But I'm warning you: you may become addicted to this soothing stuff.

Happy local shopping, everyone! I truly hope you have a Blessed Christmas, Hanukkah, Winter Solstice, Kwanzaa, or any other loving holiday that you choose to celebrate this December season.

---

* All prices in this chapter valid as of 2015. Call or check websites for current pricing.

49

CHRISTMAS POTLUCK '81

THE CHILDREN OF THE Ontko family were filled with almost as much excitement as they would be on Christmas morning. Eight-year-old Christie was going to sit on Santa's lap that night and get a present! So would her big brother (who, in her opinion, didn't deserve one) and little sister, Natalie. What a night it was going to be!

"Davey, grab an extra serving spoon outta the drawer," Mom commanded.

"Dad! Davey is squeezing me again!" Christie complained.

"David, let go of her!" Dad said as he tied Natalie's boots.

"Don't let him get your goat. Just hug him back, and he will stop. Come on, let's go! We're going to be late!" Mom said sternly. "Did you get the spoon, Davey?"

"Yup!" Davey eagerly replied.

Dad grabbed little Natalie by her mittened hand. She was the baby—the one who didn't fit into that family of dark hair, with her blonde hair and dimples. Now that she was five years old, she no longer feared the man with the white beard and red suit. All eager to get their gifts, they were full of smiles as the Ontkos piled into the '53 Chevy and headed to the Town Hall for the annual Christmas Potluck.

All the Sues had arrived: Sue Morrow, Sue Duff, and Sue Riddle. As each mom set her dish down on the table, the first Sue, Sue Morrow, Mom's high school friend, asked her, "What did you bring, Linda?"

"Tuna casserole," Mom replied. "It's Charlie's favorite. Actually, he'd eat anything!"

Sue Morrow had been creating her dish all day: chicken paprikash. She looked forward to the annual potluck. It allowed her to share her love and talent of cooking with all of the island people. Despite the fact that she had five children, she still loved finding time to provide tasty meals for others.

As the parents lit their cigarettes and Christie began to hear boring adult discussion, she quickly gathered her best friends, T.J. and Libby. "What do you think our present will be this year?" she asked them.

"Who knows? Let's sneak a cookie from the dessert table!" T.J. suggested as he scurried to the sweets. Libby and Christie immediately followed him, each grabbing a chocolate chip cookie, still warm from the oven. Mrs. Stoiber's specialty! Jay Faris and Davey joined them, and Davey promptly grabbed Christie's cookie from her hand. He took a bite, gave it back to his little sister, and then walked off laughing with Jay.

"Jerk!" Christie mumbled under her breath.

"Here," Libby said lovingly, "Take a new cookie. Throw that germy one away!"

"Gotta go," T.J. said, "My mom is calling me. Come show me what you got after we all eat!"

All three best friends separated and went to their tables with their families. There were enough Morrows to fill an entire table. The Burgesses were right beside them, but the Ontkos were at a table on the other side of the room. Christie's bottom lip stuck out as she began her usual pout, but then realized the Goazious had joined them! Sometimes the Ontkos could squeeze in another family at the end of their table, and she was glad for this. She wanted to sit next to anyone other than her big brother. Christie always liked it when she could sit next to her friends during the potluck, and Karen, the oldest of the Goaziou sisters, was there with the Ontkos. She sat beside her.

One by one, family-filled tables were instructed to circulate around the food tables to grab spoonsful of the homemade dishes. Christie only cared about the desserts. But she knew she had to eat some kind of meat—her mom would insist on it (and she wasn't at home where she was able to sneak meat to the family dog, Frieda, under the table). Christie preferred the pasta dishes; macaroni and cheese was her favorite. Hamburger helper would do, too.

The smell of cigarettes quickly filled the air. As the laughter and chatter began gaining momentum, so did the excitement of the island children, for they knew the visitor of the evening was going to be there at any moment. The double doors of the town hall would swing open with a loud creak, which would then be followed by the sound of the brass sleigh bells carried by the jolly man in his bright red suit.

Little Natalie asked anxiously, "When will he be here?"

"Soon, soon. But, he would want you to finish your dinner!" Mom answered as she guided a spoonful of corn into Natalie's mouth.

"Dad, I'm finished," Davey said. "Can I go outside and play until it's time?"

"No. Stay right here." Dad continued, "Be patient."

Davey looked over at the Faris table and shook his head from side to side, telling Jay a firm "No."

Just then, the sound of the bells echoed through the long steep staircase of the Town Hall, and a few seconds later, the creaky doors swung open.

"There he is!" Mom said with excitement.

Loud cheers came from the islanders as the youngest of the children held tightly onto their parents' necks. Little Natalie's dimples came out in full force as Santa approached the Ontko table. She wasn't even scared!

"Ho, Ho, Ho! Merry Christmas!" hollered the jolly old man through the sound of his ringing bells.

He approached the Ontko and Goaziou table, and, looking into little Christie's eyes, he asked her, "Christie, have you been a good girl this year?"

Shocked that Santa knew her name, she shyly muttered, "Uh-huh…" Santa walked on through the tables of island families "Ho-Ho-Hoing."

Christie watched as the two eldest Morrow girls were summoned to the stage to help Santa distribute the gifts. Starting with "A" last names, each island family was called up to sit on Santa's lap and receive their gifts. Each child at the potluck listened intently so they wouldn't miss their name being called. And, for the Ontkos, waiting felt like forever.

Shortly after the Naylon family received their gifts, the Ontko children were called. The nervous excitement had built up inside Christie, and she began feeling the familiar butterflies fluttering in her stomach. The stage was so big! And Santa was there! And they were going to get a few brief moments with him!

All three children were dressed in their Sunday best. Red Christmas dresses for the girls and black pants with a white shirt for Davey. His shirt had come untucked, but he didn't care. He eyed the gift that was soon to be his while Christie held onto Natalie's hand and helped her get onto the bearded man's lap.

"Smile!" Stacy said as she clicked the Polaroid camera. Her older sister, Danni, was in charge of handing out the gifts. As she did, Christie could hardly contain herself knowing there was an unknown toy inside the wrapping paper. Davey began shaking his gift, and Natalie felt the wrapped gift all over, wondering what was inside.

Gifts and wet Polaroid in hand, the three siblings walked back down the wooden steps and eagerly skipped to their family table to open their gifts. They tore into the wrapping paper while mom took picture after picture, and Dad smiled at the sight of his children's beaming faces. Strawberry Shortcake with her pink comb and sweet-smelling hair for Christie! A Star Wars Luke Skywalker figurine for Davey, and for little Natalie, a Baby Precious doll.

There weren't many families after "O," and soon the dads began folding chairs and putting the tables back underneath the old stage. Santa had gone back to the North Pole, and the moms were cleaning up the food table, making sure to grab their empty Tupperware dishes. Christie wished she could have a few more minutes to play with her new toy and socialize with her friends.

Climbing back into the '53 Chevy, Christie felt a slight sadness, even though she knew she should be grateful. Davey even helped her slide into the backseat of the car. There was so much Christmas spirit going around, and she knew there was more Christmas to be celebrated on her little island. Still to come were car rides through the snow to see all the islanders' lights, Christmas Mass, and of course, Christmas morning! And, if that weren't enough, there was always next year's Christmas Potluck to look forward to.

50

NEW YEAR'S—ISLAND STYLE

I LOVE CLIMBING THOSE STAIRS. I never tire of them. I have climbed those steps dozens and dozens of times in my life. When I was growing up, it was for Christmas potlucks and aerobics with Mrs. Valerie Mettler (when she was my gym teacher in high school.) Events such as plays, funerals, and wedding celebrations have all been held behind the old swinging doors. Then, there's that smell. The famous Town Hall smell. I love it. Now, once again, I was climbing up for my favorite reason—to celebrate. Our island New Year's Dance was being held, and the twenty-somethings of this island lovingly organized an amazing event. [From now on, I will refer to this awesome group as the young'uns.]

Cliff and I decided to invite one of our favorite couples to join us. Gordon (a.k.a. Middle Bass Gordy) and his stunning wife, Kyle. They came all the way from the Cleveland area to join in our island festivities! And, they chose to come and stay with us instead of *their* island house!

The old Town Hall doors swung open with their usual creaking sound, and I was expecting to see at least a few folks, but I think we were the very first to walk in. Julene "Jules" Market and her strapping date, Rich Myers, greeted us and took our tickets. [Such a cute couple, and so nice of them to donate their time!] We then eagerly entered the lavishly decorated Town Hall. Balloons were suspended in the netting above, awaiting the stroke of midnight to be released. There were tables filled with food surrounding the perimeter of the seating area. Streamers were added for that bit of New Year's touch, and the DJ was on the old stage waiting to fill the place with sound. I guess it was my excitement that made us leave our dinner at Tipper's a little early, but I was so ready to be a part of this old island tradition once again—and to show off "my" Town Hall to the Middle Bassers. Yes, we were the first to arrive, but soon the place became a mecca for the young and old and in-between; a celebration, island-style!

We took a seat around a table that was covered with things I cannot eat—homemade cookies. I heard that the lovely Linda Rence helped make them. [How nice of her!] I love to bake also, but eating them is the problem. So, take a bite I did not. Instead, I took a sip of my favorite cocktail—a Margarita with lots of lime, already mixed and inside my to-go container from home. It was BYOB, after all. I meandered over to the tables overflowing with more food: meatballs, chips and salsa, and other delicious things that I swore I wasn't going to eat. But I did. They were just too yummy to pass up.

More people began to filter in—thank God! I had talked up this evening so much to my guests, and I didn't want to let them down. I told them *anyone who was anyone* would be there.

The music began playing. I was crossing my fingers for an Indigo Girls song, or at least some from John Denver. But this young DJ had other plans. At times there were loud thumps and bumps that tested the mettle of that old Town Hall. Lights flashing all around shown brightly out of the old windows, making me wonder if the mainlanders could see the colors. It was the DJ's attempt to get the people moving, I guess. He was only doing his job. I just sipped my extra lime Margarita and tried to forget about the blinding light. I guess the young'uns like that sorta music and bright light effects. More people filtered in—so many! The young, the newly turned 21-year-olds, and their college friends. People from my generation and my mom's, too! It was so great seeing everyone come through those old doors. At one time, there was even a line to get in. I think half the island was in there. Julene and her hot date at the ticket counter had their work cut out for them!

As I watched the islanders enter the party, I decided to join my handsome date on the dance floor. I'm going to let you in on a little secret—I cannot dance. I know, I know, who would've thought? However, it was New Year's Eve, and I was going to try my best. Slow dancing—easy. I just have to follow fancy-footed Cliff. Fast dancing—I just try to hide behind everyone else on the dance floor. So, if you were there and happened to see me, I sincerely apologize. I tell ya who was a great fast dancer—Mrs. Gordon Barr, that's who! She was out there in her glittery black top going crazy! That woman can *move*! Maybe she can give me lessons someday....

The DJ got better as the night moved toward the New Year. He even played Michael Jackson, and I found myself dancing alongside former students. Now, how many teachers can say *that*? Well, I guess on Put-in-Bay, we can. My mom was in attendance, as was Mr. John Ladd, her former teacher. I did see Dr. Trisler—and she was my teacher! Hopefully, she didn't see my missteps on the dance floor. [Love that Dr. Trisler!]

But there wasn't just dancing at this awesome party; there was a place for photo-ops, too! Jeff Koehler loved that. I witnessed smiles, laughter, and fun from all ages at the picture area. What a creative bunch those young'uns are! They had made little paper hats on sticks that we placed above our heads to make it look as though we were wearing them. There were little mustaches, too, so we could make Gordy look like he hadn't shaved. I'm sure in the pictures that were taken that night, we all looked ravishing! The realistic pictures, complete with amusing props, will be a keepsake for sure. Great job, Young'uns!

What I loved about this dance were the multi-generational folks in attendance. Some had just turned 21, while others were approaching 71. It was just wonderful to see all the islanders, cottagers, Middle Bassers, and college kids there! It's a great tradition that I hope to see for many years to come. To Jacob Market and his gang of young'uns for organizing this great event—thank you!

I apologize that I didn't help clean up the next day, but now that I've hit the age of 40, I'm too old for that hard work. Plus, I was very busy making an organic breakfast for my Middle Basser guests while sipping my Bloody Mary.

51

ONE LAST SNOWFALL

SOFTLY FALLING THROUGH THE sky, the flakes reach the ground and cover it, instantly changing the gray look of the island into a bright, white glow. Resting on every single branch and leftover twig from the fall, the white stuff beautifully outlines nature. Each year, the island gets to experience one final gorgeous snowfall. Usually occurring in the month of March, this last hurrah of winter is frustrating to those who are anxious for spring to come, and, as much as I'm a lover of the spring season, this last snow is somehow "allowed" by me. I know that spring is on its way, and I don't actually mind the last snow because I know it is the *last* snow.

Weather. It's what we islanders talk about. A lot. Now, I don't have control over it, but if I did, I would have about three inches of that beautiful, heavy, wet snow fall every Christmas Eve and Christmas Day. Then, maybe a little more on New Year's Eve—right at midnight. Big, fluffy flakes. And the temperature would hover right around the freezing mark so that the snow would stay wet—perfect for building a snowman and a good temperature for sticking to the tree branches as well as the mums and hydrangeas that I didn't cut down in the fall. Oh, so pretty!

Then, after Christmas and New Year's Eve, I would boost the temperature. I would make plenty of sunshine so that daily walks could be taken without my fingers freezing off. The lake would be open all winter long—easy for the ferries to continue running. I would throw in a good Nor'easter once a month until April. These windy days would fall on the weekends, allowing me an excuse each month to stay inside, under the covers of my warm bed, and write stories all day, only taking breaks for episodes of *Scandal*. Oh, those Nor'easters! In my happy world of controlling the weather, winter would be only a brief blink in the year, and I would get my windy days inside.

Wait—I think that's what we got this year! Or, at least, pretty close. My brother, Davey, got to experience a weekend of ice fishing, so he was happy. Shawn Dages also informed me of his four days of heaven on the ice. My nieces got to go ice-skating, and I even gave my old rusted ice skates to my little sister to use. [She's a regular Dorothy Hamil, folks.] And, although it didn't snow on Christmas Day, I did see some pretty snow in February. I didn't manage daily power walks but did get up many mornings to watch gorgeous sunrises while walking safely along the monument seawall, and I got to listen to open, flowing water lapping up along the shore. There were only a few times when the stillness of the frozen lake surrounded me. After the coldest spell of the winter, I was able to leave for a visit to Gordon and Kyle Barr's place in the Florida sunshine during winter break from school. So, in retrospect, I only had to freeze for several weeks instead of many months this winter.

Please, Patty Bauer, no more playing with that magical snow globe of yours. I will make a deal with you and allow *one last* snowfall, and all the open water for miles, during the month of March—not April, like the storm my great uncle, Earl remembered. I want to see all of the cottage owners here each and every weekend. Pronto. Come back, Christine (Booker) Keyes—and bring those cute children with you! [Especially my little Penelope.] Hurry up, Joan French! Sally and Jim, I miss you! I want my water running without worry of freezing pipes, and I am eager to see the first sign of tulips as they peak their new shoots through the mulched leaves. Oh, and I really want our boats to run on schedule. Who else is with me?

52

POSITIVELY PUT-IN-BAY

Y HIGH SCHOOL YEARBOOK reads, "We Kristin Altoff, Paul Riddle, Tom Yost, and Shawn Evans do hereby will to Christie Ontko: one more thing to complain about." Ouch. The only thing my classmates could write about me in all our years together was that I was a complainer. Wow. This wasn't really something to be proud of as I passed through my transition into adulthood. I know yearbooks are supposed to be funny and a little sarcastic, but this "will" left me feeling not so well.

I was defensive at first. Then, I was angry. Most of all, I was embarrassed that others thought this of me. This characteristic that my classmates ascribed to me stuck with me throughout my adult life. I strongly believe I began to change after I read that comment from my classmates 23 years ago.

Gandhi was reported to have said, "If we could change ourselves, the tendencies in the world would also change. As a man changes his own nature, so does the attitude of the world change towards him."

Recently, I made a decision. After hearing negative things in the news about our little island, I chose to change my outlook. Instead of complaining about this and that and getting caught up in all the negativity, I decided to follow Gandhi's advice, as well as learn from what my classmates had taught me. I began a "Positive Put-in-Bay Post Per Day" on my Facebook page. Here are a few:

- Day #4: **Water.** We are surrounded by water. This is so cool. If you're ever feeling down, all ya have to do is go for a short walk, maybe even just ten minutes— soon, you'll see Lake Erie! It is constantly changing, creating a most beautiful backdrop for Put-in-Bay.

- Day #6: **Safety.** Kids living and going to school here can walk or bike to school in complete safety. Through wooded paths, bike paths, or just on our roads. Our kids are safe and sound.

- Day #7: **Forgiveness.** We are a small community, and because of this, we bump into each other often. At the grocery store, the post office, or the gas station. Sometimes, we bump into an ex or someone we've had words with. This allows forgiveness to occur faster. This allows us to remain human with each other. Forgiveness—one of the great things about this little island.

- Day #8: **Opportunity.** I have been fortunate to start and operate my dream healing business! Here today all day!!—at Freshwater Retreat, Freshwater Sensations LLC.

- Day #9: **Historical Weekend.** Or whatever they're calling it now. I love this weekend!

- Day #10: **Closeness**. I get to teach in the same school both my daughters attended. [Meredith is still there—at this writing, a junior in high school.] In a small community, where our school is a pivotal part of who we are, I have been allowed access to my daughters whenever they needed me. I've been allowed to comfort them when they fell down on the playground or sign a parent form on the fly. I've been allowed to see my two daughters in an element of their childhood—in the hallways, out on the playground, or even just warming up for a run in cross-country. A great gift and comfort to me. This may be the most positive thing for me about this little island.

- Day #11: **No Judgement**. My Christmas decorations are still not inside the attic. This morning, I noticed I've been using a Halloween potholder for at least a year. [But it's almost Halloween again, so I'm in luck!] Not one person on my street would even judge me. Such nice people, we have here. Nice neighbors and good folks!

- Day #12: **Perry's Monument**. The view is so beautiful from up on top. It stands tall in our sky and stands for *peace*, and that just makes me so happy!

- Day #13: **Lunch Hour**. At our school there is no cafeteria, allowing us all to do our own thing for lunch. Many of our kids go home to eat with their families, and teachers can do the same! Some enjoy a meal at one of the island's great restaurants. A way to reconnect and a very positive thing!

• Day #14. **Fall**. A beautiful time of year with the oh-so-purple grapes; the leaves slowly turning auburn; and the red, yellow, and gold mums in full bloom. A more relaxing vibe spreads through the people, and it's just kinda nice.

• Day #15: **Activities**. Fishing, swimming, boating, ice-skating, ice-boating, ice-fishing, and watching sunsets. All really great things we can do here because of beautiful Lake Erie. If you haven't ever seen a sunset off the West Shore, you *must* do this before you die. Seriously. Go to the ramp to do this. If you don't know where the ramp is, just ask someone.

• Day #16: **Jobs**. There are so many jobs here for so many people! My daughter, Anna—always great to see her—came home to work for Chris Krueger, and I'm grateful to the business owners who employ our local kids and help them financially throughout their lives. We have a great local economy!

• Day #17: **Comradery**. I was at the Post Office today, and Cathy van Liere needed a ride home because she had just dropped her car off at the garage. "Christie, can you give me a ride home?" she asked. "Sure, Cathy! But, I have to mail out these packages first. Can you wait a minute or two?" I responded. I proceeded to load up my boxes with shirts that didn't fit, fill out the "return" labels, packaged everything up, and then waited for J.R. to weigh it all. [He was very quick, I might add.] Cathy just waited patiently. *Where on earth* can you do this? *Where else* can someone just ask for a ride, chitchat about returning items bought online that don't fit, and then get a safe ride home? I don't really talk to or see Cathy van Liere that often, but it is *so* nice that we live in a place where people don't have to be best friends to help one another out. I love it!

- #18: **The *Gazette***. Jeff Koehler just asked me for my October article. I'm on deadline. I love being "on deadline." It makes me feel like such a real writer....

If you are a recovering complainer, like me, then I challenge you to try it. Try positivity. It's everywhere you look, and it makes each day so much better.

Those four classmates in 1991 helped me to see something I didn't see—or didn't want to see—about myself. However, this "complaining Christie" didn't truly leave me until I was much older. On occasion, she will still begin to show her negative little head, and she has to bite her tongue or refrain from writing her unfiltered thoughts in this little island paper. I have never forgotten the "will," but now it just reminds me of how far I've come. My classmates taught me a great lesson a long time ago, and for that, I am eternally grateful.

53

WHAT DO YOU WANT?

’VE BEEN SEEING RABBITS all over the place lately. Dead rabbits, too. In fact, my cat, Charlie, caught one, and we believe it made him very ill. So I decided to look up the symbolism of "rabbit." According to Scott Foglesong, creator of Medicine Cards, "The keynote here is: what you resist will persist! What you fear most is what you will become."

Whether or not you believe in symbols, I feel this fits what's going on right now on our little place called Put-in-Bay. Fear. Lots of it. Dear Readers, I have debated about writing on this topic. But, alas, my boss Jeff Koehler has asked me to. Maybe I just needed his permission to get a little political in my column this month because I usually shy away from writing about such things. However, I have always held strong opinions and, like generations of my family on this island, I care very deeply about Put-in-Bay.

I would say that many of us have fears about what happened this past "Christmas in July." We've seen the pictures on Facebook, heard the stories from business owners, and have even seen things with our own eyes that we never thought we'd see on this precious little island that many of us call home. Or, maybe this past July just brought up not-so-happy memories of long ago on the island. I've personally talked to many people: employees, bar owners, locals—both year-round and summer—and tourists who were here that weekend in July. After listening and processing it all, here's what I've come up with.

What are our fears? What did the past "Christmas in July" bring? Let's get to it.

I believe that the worst fears for our island's future are: extreme partying/drinking, which can lead to rioting; not enough law enforcement or sufficient time to get reinforcements because of the geography; bodily harm or even death to tourists, locals, and workers; and worries that our island will become a place where visitors don't want to come anymore.

They won't want to travel on our ferries or dine in our wonderful restaurants. They'll decide not to raise their little babies here. And those fears bring up other questions: what if the island becomes a place strictly for those who enjoy corruption, drug abuse, and extreme partying? What if we lose many of our year-round residents? What if all our long-time summer cottage owners get fed up and sell?

Our charming little island that allows people to be who they are and has forever been a wonderful getaway and a place for tourists to come and release all their mainland worries will no longer exist.

The Medicine Cards web page I read continued to discuss what to do with fear, "When you encounter a rabbit, you must stop talking about horrible things happening and get rid of the "what if" in your vocabulary. This card may signal a time of worrying about the future or trying to exercise control over that which is not yet in form: the future. Stop now!"

But how do we stop the fear?

By focusing on what we *do* want now. "But, Christie," you

may say, "Everyone wants different things. How do we make a happy island for everyone?"

I would reply with, "What are the things we can all agree upon? Prosperity. Tourism. A clean Lake Erie. Love. Community. Safety. Happiness. Longevity. Abundance." I believe these things are at the core of what most everyone living here wants.

I've read the long posts on Facebook. We must *stop* the blaming.

If business owner A wants to attract clients ABC, then *let* him. If business owner Z wants to attract XYZ, then let *him*. If you are on the "side" of A, then create or help promote more businesses like A. And, if you are on the "side" of Z, then create or promote more like that. *However*, both A and Z must agree to observe the laws—both state and local. We are a society that needs laws for the safety, happiness, and security of everyone and ultimately, laws help us continue to get what we want.

Stop the inner-island fighting with one another!

Focus on what you want and hold onto this idea. Be like a dog that won't let go of his bone. Create more of what you want, and you will get it. "Ask, and it shall be given you; seek, and ye shall find; knock, and it shall be opened unto you." I'm sure many of you have heard that before…yes, I've just quoted the Bible.

Change is going to happen; it always does. However, we must all take a step back and look at the changes that have occurred, look into our own mirrors and see how we have played or not played a part in those changes. Learn from errors and fix what can be mended.

I believe the past July's events brought abundance to the downtown businesses. It brought people—lots of them—and money. We usually think of "lots of people" as being a very good thing. I have heard that most bars that weekend broke records.

I've also heard that even though money was made, the owners of these places realize that the craziness among the abundance of visitors was too much. *Way* too much.

Even though I do not agree with the promotion or celebration of "Christmas in July," I can agree that it brought prosperity to the island. Not all of us benefitted from the large crowds (including my wellness shop at zero dollars), but I can accept that. I did, however have a very peaceful house at half-capacity due to my strict rules and regulations. I do not expect every Saturday to be record-breaking.

But I *will not* accept the desecration of my island home, nor the other unlawful activities that were witnessed by many of us. Those activities are against the law—laws that were created by the State of Ohio and the United States of America to keep our children, families, and guests safe.

Am I angry at our police force? No. I believe they "allowed" these behaviors simply because they knew they were out-numbered. As a result, they showed their presence, but couldn't arrest everyone, simply because there were too many to be arrested. I believe they did their best that Saturday night in July, given the number of people on the island. There is a solution for this: bring more police and security. Even if we *all* have to pay up.

We all benefit from tourism. Even if you aren't the owner of a business, if it weren't for tourism, there would be no reason for people to come here to live. Remember when, at the beginning of Put-in-Bay's history, people tried making a living as sheep farmers? That didn't work out so well…. I benefit from tourism even as a teacher. Who works in the bars, restaurants, and bed and breakfasts? You. Me. Then we have children, and those children need a school. See?

We must learn from this past summer and be more prepared next year. If we continue doing the same thing—complaining, blaming, and criticizing one another, then we will implode. Remember…what do *you* want???

I am through complaining and am suggesting some changes here. I moved my retreat business three years ago from the mainland back to my island home and am finishing the raising of my two daughters here. I have accepted that our island is known to many as a "Party Island." I don't think I have the power to change the minds of thousands of people about this. However, the word "party" can mean a different thing to different people. How about having a party with respect and dignity? How about a party with limits within the law? How about a party with some relaxation or a nature walk the next day? Maybe even a party with some time for shopping or learning about our island history? I'm not against alcohol; in fact, I love it! I love dry red wine, yummy tequila, and even love a good whiskey that has aged in its barrel for many years. But, I'm aware that when I partake in drinking, I must follow laws.

Remember the quote from the movie *Field of Dreams*? "Build it, and they will come." Let's remember what it is we are building. What and who are we attracting? What type of visitors do we want? What impression do we want to leave on our tourists? Again, I ask you to think about this long and hard, what do you want? Trust me. You'll get it. We got this past "Christmas in July," folks. If you don't like it, then change your focus to something different.

54

TEN WAYS

'VE ALWAYS SAID THAT there are ten ways that living and working on an island will ruin you for life. Now that the season in the Lake Erie Islands is well on its way, the summer workers are like a colony of ants working together for one common goal: to create an amazing season for the island guests. With jobs galore including, but not limited to, working on a ferry, sharing your talents on a stage, or making delicious concoctions for visitors, the Lake Erie Islands are unique and special in their employment opportunities. Not only are the best jobs going to make you money for college and possibly become your career, but some of the people you encounter will become forever friends, and you'll have experiences like nothing the mainland could deliver. Work a seasonal job on a Lake Erie Island, and you'll never be the same. Trust me.

A FERRY CAPTAIN

My grandfather was known as Captain Parker, and my father and husband are both captains on Lake Erie. Even at 80 years old with years of retirement under his belt, my dad is still known today as Capt. Charlie Tuna, the kind ferry captain who let the kids blow the Miller Ferry horn. In this job, you're instantly loved, and you'll learn how to handle both rough and calm days on Lake Erie. You even get to wear really nice shirts! If you choose to become a Captain, you will work for hours to learn the rules of the water and have every weather app on your phone. Whether it's working for Jet Xpress, Miller Boat Line, The Boardwalk Water Taxi Service, or operating your own charter service, this is a job for water lovers! Take a look online at some of the career choices associated with this at:

- Miller Ferries, service to Put-in-Bay and Middle Bass Island
- Jet Express, service to Put-in-Bay, Kelleys Island, and Cedar Point
- Freshwater Charters, fishing charter in Put-in-Bay

DOCK MASTER

Speaking of the water and boats, if you love them but get seasick (like I do), maybe you'll want to choose the job of helping those boats dock safely. You will learn how to tie crazy awesome knots and must have a good boatside manner. I've never done this job myself, but my friends (and big brother Davey) did work on those docks and told me all about it. They had information on boats of every shape, size, and name. They became friends with many of the boat owners, which allowed them perks such as free boating excursions. Dock Masters also earn plenty of money for college and beyond. For more information on this type of employment, contact the Tourism Bureau at:

- VISITPUTINBAY.COM

BARTENDER

When speaking of expenses for higher learning, let's not forget about the bars that need tending. I was a bartender once upon a looooong time ago at the world-famous Beer Barrel

Saloon. That summer, I could afford the most amazing clothing, all while paying my tuition to Bowling Green. Yes, you make great tips. However, you must learn to put up with "interesting" people and work the longest hours ever. [HINT: get the best shoes money can buy, or else you'll have achy feet and legs every night.] The best part of my experience working there was the lifelong friends I made. Hop over to Kelleys or Middle Bass Islands, too. They have some neat bars there, as well.

- Beer Barrel Saloon, Put-In-Bay
- J.F. Walleye's, Middle Bass
- The Casino, Kelleys Island

BNB PROPRIETOR

After years of teaching school and working various other summer jobs on the island of Put-in-Bay, I decided to follow in my mom's footsteps and open a BnB. This experience has continued to surprise and delight me! Not only do I get to offer a classy experience to summer visitors, but I'm also making friends with many of them who come back year after year. It's truly humbling to make up beds with extra special care, clean toilets, and create a space of relaxation for my guests. If you like to clean, love people, and want to offer a restful place for visitors, like I do, I highly recommend this job! It gives me a sense of great pride, and I think it could do the same for you, too.

- Freshwater Retreat, Put-In-Bay
- English Pines, Put-In-Bay
- House on Huntington Lane, for an Irish flair on Kelleys Island

INTERN FOR THE LAKE ERIE ISLANDS CONSERVANCY

Another job that gives back is one where you get to do all sorts of outdoorsy things for the islands. As an intern, you get to help out in so many ways! Hands-on with educational programs, being outside in nature, and constantly promoting land conservation. If you're lucky, maybe *you* can obtain this position in the future.

- Lake Erie Islands Conservancy

GENERAL STORE

They work in air-conditioned comfort, get the first pick of all the fresh produce, and get to rearrange rows of canned goods. Seriously, this job would be *fun*!

However, I've also noticed those women and men stand on their feet for long hours so that you and I can buy our necessary items. [Thank them the next time you visit.] I also see them having tons of fun with the customers, chatting, and getting to know everyone by name—even all the summer workers! If it weren't for our Put-in-Bay and Middle Bass Island General Stores, we'd have empty island cupboards.

CHEF

We have delicious food throughout the islands, thanks to these creative folks. From a full lobster dinner at The Boardwalk to a scrumptious hamburger at Mossbacks (both on Put-in-Bay), our island chefs enjoy working with food and crafting delicious meals for you and me. Thank goodness for people like this! [I love to eat out!] Here are a few places, all in Put-in-Bay, where you can apply to work for next season:

- The Forge
- The Boardwalk
- Mossbacks Island Bar & Grill

WAITER/WAITRESS

In order to get your food, you must have a multi-tasking,

high-energy human to deliver it to you, like Sandy at Tipper's. I've done this work, as have many in my family before me. It is a belief of mine that everyone—and I mean, *everyone*—should do this job at least for a day. This job is hard, but the benefits are pretty amazing, too. Some of my most favorite memories are of the summer as a morning waitress at The Snack House or serving lunches at The Goat. I met people from all over the world and made great tips, too!

- Frosty's
- Reel Bar
- The Goat Soup and Whiskey

ENTERTAINER/ARTIST

Some of us are born with musical talent. Pat Dailey, Bob Gatewood, Ray Fogg, and Jamison Smith are just a few of the fabulous entertainers of Put-in-Bay. You can make a living at this, folks! But, be prepared for hours and hours of practice and commitment to your craft. If you enjoy being on stage and sharing your artistic flair with others, then this may be the job for you. I think we have more budding singers on the horizon, too. Just ask Chad Hughes to sing a tune for you. I recall when his father, Greg, opened up for Pat Dailey at The Beer Barrel. Check out Pat's FaceBook page at FACEBOOK.COM/ PATDAILEYPHD. For more inspiration, go to:

- FLYINJAYS.COM
- BOBGATEWOOD.COM
- RAYFOGG.NET

COLUMNIST FOR THE *PUT-IN-BAY GAZETTE*

I wish I could say my *Gazette* press pass gets me backstage into my favorite musical venues, but sadly, it doesn't. Wait, I *think* I could ask the above artists for a backstage pass.... [Indigo

Girls *will* allow me backstage someday...wait a minute! Rascal Flatts?] But, all the backstage stuff aside, writing for the island paper over the years has taught me so much about the island I call home. More importantly, it's made me truly appreciate my life here as an Island Girl, spreading the love of Put-in-Bay and the Lake Erie Islands, and in doing so, gaining new perspectives into my own life. Working on a Lake Erie Island *does* change you: it spoils you and ruins you for other places. And I highly recommend it.

55

WHAT SHE MEANS TO ME

TWENTY-SEVEN YEARS AGO, I wrote for the *Gazette* for the very first time. It was a commentary written during my senior year of high school, and I recall it being a pretty intense one because of all the comments I got from readers after I wrote it. I remember writing about how amazing the island is and how I wish everyone could see it from my eyes. I recall being defensive of my island, my beautiful Put-in-Bay, writing about how you don't have to come here and party-hearty, but you can come here and revel in her beauty and partake in family-fun activities, too!

That was in 1991, and now I'm feeling the same way. Why am I always feeling the need to defend my best friend, Put-in-Bay?

People come to our island for many reasons, and everyone has his or her own idea of *what* Put-in-Bay is really all about. For some, it's an island of release, letting go of mainland troubles and taking a breather for a weekend. With that "release" sometimes comes heavy alcohol consumption and abnormal behavior from some of our visitors. Others simply relax by camping with their families at the State Park or roasting marshmallows along the cliffs while watching the sunset. Then there are the homeowners who began as tourists, like my husband, Cliff. For others who have lived here their entire lives, like me, it's been my home—for five generations of Parkers—but who's counting? Like any friend with multiple personalities, Put-in-Bay has been both a source of contention and one of affection for me. At times in my life, I've tried to leave her behind to get away from all the negativity she can sometimes bring. When in high school, I was going off to see the world, explore, and meet others who share my thoughts on all things spiritual and earthy. BGSU wasn't very far away, but after getting my teaching degree, I realized that I needed my island friend more than ever, with a new baby named Anna on the way. I was then offered a teaching job here and never left, until two winters ago when Maui called my name.

What I think I had to realize was that Put-in-Bay was more than just *my* home. I have to share her with many others who have different expectations of her. That's why she attracts all backgrounds of people looking for different types of vacation activities. That's what makes her so special; she can make anyone feel at home. I don't think we'll ever all see her the exact same way, as even my own perception of her changes from day to day and year to year. But my feelings for her remain the same. I love her like a crazy old aunt who changes her hats too often.

I encourage *you*, dear reader, to think about what the island means to you. You're probably reading this because a part of you loves Put-in-Bay. If you truly love her as I do, let's try to get some therapy for her. She might be confused and doesn't know who she is. Or, maybe she doesn't mind being something different to each and every one of us, and I'm just going to have to be okay with her changing personalities. Whoever she is, I will always love her. She has brought me so much, and I'll continue to do my best to take care of and give back to her in every way I can.

56

FORGIVENESS

THE LONGER I LIVE here, the more I hate it that everyone knows me and knows my "stuff." However, the longer I live here, the more I love it that everyone knows my stuff. My errors and experiences make me human. It makes me understand someone else's stuff when he or she comes to me for Life Coaching. It makes me a better mom, friend, and person, in general. There is an old saying, "Those who live in glass houses shouldn't throw stones." So true.

On this little island which I've called home for the last 47 years, I've learned many things, such as how to carefully navigate an ex-boyfriend, ex-husband, or even an ex-friend. I've learned strategies that mainland people living in large cities would never have to put to use. Such as going to the post office—a room that is only about 20 feet long and six feet wide—and how to "nicely" bump into an ex. And I mean *literally* bump into an ex, then laugh about it after getting my mail out of my box.

Forgiveness is a great gift, if we're ready to receive it. I've learned it, but at times have regressed and become angry again. As I said, I'm human. I've witnessed the most amazing acts of forgiveness and love, living here. Frankly, I'm amazed by it all!

Despite all our other human faults, I would say we island folks are pretty good at this forgiveness thing.

But maybe you still need to work on this? At times I could definitely use a refresher course in this healing work of forgiveness. Take this quiz and find out where you stand on the topic.

1. You see an ex on the road as you pass by; what do you do?

   a. Look the other way. (1 pt.)

   b. Lovingly wave in your usual fashion. (3 pts.)

   c. Wave eagerly, possibly with a little bit of underlying sarcasm. (2 pts.)

2. When in the grocery store and shopping for groceries, you notice a fellow islander with whom you just don't see eye-to-eye. So, you…

   a. Put your shoulders back, stand a bit taller, and look down at your grocery list. (2 pts.)

   b. Smile. Then get on with your grocery shopping. (3 pts.)

   c. Dodge them by pretending to shop for something frozen. You stick your head inside the freezer, picking up packaged meats and pretending to read what is on each label. "Maybe they won't notice me and will get their stuff and get outta here—fast!" (1 pt.)

3. When in line at the grocery store, you turn around to see an ex (friend or lover) standing there with their arms full of food, waiting to pay. How do you react?

   a. "Hey! Do you wanna put your stuff down?" and then quickly move your groceries down on the counter to make room for theirs. (3 pts.)

   b. You promptly turn back around and pretend they aren't there. You may even think mean thoughts to yourself about the food they're buying. (1 pt.)

    c. Nervously continue on in the line, but if they say something to you first, you will respond. (2 pts.)

4. You've just signed up for a volunteer position and notice your ex-friend's name is on the list, too.

    a. You are bummed. Can't you do anything on the island without them being there, too? (1 pt.)

    b. "This is great! Maybe we can patch up our differences and come together for this great island cause," you think to yourself and truly mean it. (3 pts.)

    c. You think, "Well, this is going to be awkward! Maybe I shouldn't have joined." (2 pts.)

5. You are out to dinner with your significant other. Your ex comes in with their new significant other. What do you do?

    a. "Let's hurry up, eat, and get outta here!" you say to your current love. (1 pt.)

    b. "Hey, how is it going, (name of ex)? Aren't you going to introduce me to this lovely person you're with?" You say this without any sarcasm and with a genuine hopefulness that your ex is happy. (3 pts.)

    c. Eat dinner, but inside you're uncomfortable. You're hopeful that things will get better as time passes. (2 pts.)

score 5-9: You still need to work on forgiveness. But don't beat yourself up; at times in my life, I would not even have been able to *take* a quiz like this. I would've cried at the thought of an ex or become red with anger at a person who disagreed with me. But, you'll grow. You'll forgive. You'll let go, too. Trust me.

score 10-19: You're on your way to forgiving, but still have some hurt to work through. It's okay—time really does help with this. Hang in there. We all digress sometimes. Learning to forgiven takes time.

score 20-25: You know that this forgiveness stuff doesn't just happen overnight, but you've allowed yourself to work through it. You truly wish for everyone to be able to just let it all go and move on. You send love to all of your ex-lovers and hope that they are happy. When you see an island person with whom you disagree on the politics of things, you don't take it personally, allowing everyone to believe what he or she wants.

I wish I could say that I've reached a score of 25, but it takes more time than that. The responses in the above quiz are things I've actually done, felt, and acted out. And that's why I'm still here—because I am learning how to let things go and getting better at it all the time. I am far from perfect, but I am willing to work towards becoming a better person. Lastly, I do hope that all my ex-friends, lovers, and people with whom I don't see eye-to-eye have forgiven me…or at least are working on it, too.

Sometimes in life, things don't turn out the way you think they will, which has happened to me far too often. However, I must have faith that the Universe has better plans in store for me. Just as I never, ever thought I'd still be living on Put-in-Bay as an adult, I'd say my life has been filled with magical surprises and extraordinary experiences. I am meant to still be here, at the age of almost 48, living the life of a Lake Erie Island Girl. And as life will forever be evolving, relationships will also change. It is my belief that people are meant to be in one's life for as long a time as is necessary for each person's development and growth. Cliff, the man I wrote about in many of my stories and with whom I share some wonderful memories, is no longer my partner. Although we have decided to go our separate ways, I know that, wherever life takes him, he will be bold, strong, and having the time of his life.

And, so will I.

Beginnings of a dock

Downtown Put-in-Bay, sometime in the 50s

Grandpa Alfred

Grape pickers

Grampa Parker ice fishing

Shanties on the shore

Put-in-Bay races ca. 1950s

Erie Isle — top on

Work on Langram road

The "Erie Isle" and "Yankee Clipper" at sea